BUILDING AN EFFECTIVE CONGREGATION COUNCIL

Susan Carloss

Augsburg Fortress, Minneapolis

CONTENTS

BUILDING AN EFFECTIVE CONGREGATION COUNCIL

This resource has been developed by Augsburg Fortress and the Division for Congregational Ministries of the Evangelical Lutheran Church in America. DCM Project Coordinator: Michael R. Rothaar. We are grateful for the collaboration of the Office of the Secretary of the ELCA and the Rev. Harold B. Everson, Division for Church in Society.

Editors: Beth Ann Gaede and Louise Lystig
Cover design: Connie Helgeson-Moen
Page design: Carol Evans-Smith

Bible quotations, unless otherwise indicated, are from the New Revised Standard Version Bible, copyright © 1989, Division of Christian Education of the National Council of Churches in the United States of America. Used by permission.

Excerpt from *The Book of Concord,* translated and edited by Theodore G. Tappert, copyright © 1959 Fortress Press.

Excerpt from *The Small Catechism by Martin Luther in Contemporary English with Lutheran Book of Worship text (1979 Edition),* copyright © 1960, 1968.

INTRODUCTION

PURPOSE OF THIS BOOK

Serving on the Congregation Council can be a satisfying and personally rewarding ministry. Often a person who serves on the council experiences a renewal of faith as she or he responds to God's call to leadership, faithfully fulfilling specific duties and responsibilities.

Certainly another important benefit of serving on the council is the sense of community that grows between the people who work together as leaders of a congregation.

This handbook offers members of the Congregation Council and their pastors an opportunity to examine their responsibilities and relationships, and the ministry of congregational leadership to which they are called.

Building an Effective Congregation Council can help congregational leaders to:

- grow in their understanding of God's mission and the church;
- envision new possibilities for building a leadership team;
- develop skills in planning and making leadership decisions.

This book provides an interactive study and will address questions like these:

- How is leadership on the Congregation Council different from leadership in other organizations?
- What is the Evangelical Church in America (ELCA), and how is our congregation connected to it?
- What are the duties of the Congregation Council member?
- Who will be serving on the council?
- How can a council make effective leadership decisions together?

The book is divided into twelve chapters. These chapters will explore the steps in building an effective Congregation Council.

USING THIS RESOURCE

Format

This handbook is addressed to the individual council member, but it will be most effective if it is used by a group of council members who can discuss ideas and share insights. Be flexible, focusing on material that meets your needs and those of your group. Everything you need is in this handbook, and each group participant should have a copy.

Each chapter will include the following:

Overview   This will describe the topics to be covered in the session.

Objectives   These are the learning goals for the session.

Information   Depending on how you will use this handbook, the material covered in the chapters could be presented by a facilitator, or each member of your council could read the material beforehand. Chapters might include two types of activities, which are identified by the color boxes:

- *Group discussion*   Your group is encouraged to complete the activity, study, or discussion described. Individual, small group, and large group activities are included.
- *Personal reflection*   Occasionally you will be invited to reflect individually on questions.

Looking Ahead   This describes resources you will need for the next chapter. You might be asked to read these materials, in addition to the chapter itself, before your meeting.

Resources   Listed here are books and other resources that cover a topic addressed in the chapter in greater depth or from a different perspective.

Approaches to the Study

This handbook can be used in several ways:

Council Development   Set aside time to use one chapter at each monthly meeting of your Congregation Council for a year.

Each chapter can be completed by a group in twenty minutes to half an hour. You can shorten sessions by having council members read material ahead of time and by using only some of the group activities. Those sections that are not used for the year's study can then be incorporated into a council retreat or saved for council development in a second year.

One of your Congregation Council members or your pastor could lead the study, inviting those who like to read to explore resources listed at the end of each chapter and facilitating group work by simply following the written instructions.

Individual Orientation   Some people who are elected to council leadership are new to the Lutheran church or unfamiliar with the specific responsibilities of council leaders in your congregation. Give this handbook to new council members as part of an orientation to the Congregation Council. You might suggest several chapters to be read fairly early as they begin their work. Group activities could be handled by a group of newly elected members, or the activities might be incorporated into the entire council's agenda as council development.

If this handbook is given to individuals as an introduction to the Congregation Council, the congregation president or pastor should follow up with the council member and respond to any questions or comments the new member might have.

Another idea might be for the nominating committee to share this handbook with prospective council members before the congregation election, so nominees will understand the leadership position to which they would be elected.

Building as Effective Congregation Council also could be included in a council notebook given to every member of the council.

Congregation Council Retreat   The content of this book can be set into a one-day, overnight, or weekend Congregation Council retreat. The material could be divided into seven sessions, which would fit into a overnight retreat like this:

Evening, Day One

7:00 P.M. Opening Worship

7:15 P.M. Welcome, introductions, and announcements
Sharing expectations

7:30 P.M. Sessions 1 and 2: "Understanding the ELCA"

8:15 P.M. Break

8:30 P.M. Sessions 3 and 4: "Duties of the Congregation Council"

9:15 P.M. Evening Devotions

9:30 P.M. Refreshments and Fellowship

Day Two

8:45 A.M. Morning Worship

9:00 A.M. Council members select one of three group studies:
Session 5: "Models for Your Council's Structure"
Session 6: "Your Role as a Council Member"
Session 12: "Communicating with the Congregation"

9:30 A.M. Discussing group studies

10:00 A.M. Break

10:30 A.M. Session 7: "Leadership Styles and Group Dynamics"

11:00 A.M. Break

11:15 A.M. Session 8: "Becoming a Leadership Team"

12:00 A.M. Lunch

1:00 P.M. Sessions 9 and 10: "Making Decisions" (in groups of three)

1:45 P.M. Break

2:00 P.M. Session 11: "Planning and Goal Setting"

2:30 P.M. Group Discussion: "Hopes and Dreams for our Congregation Council"

3:15 P.M. Closing Worship

This schedule could be adapted to a one-day or weekend retreat. You also might use half of this book for one retreat and the remaining material at another retreat or throughout the year as council development.

Synod Training Event for Congregation Councils   A synod might provide a day-long or overnight workshop for Congregation Council members. The workshop could be open to several members from each congregation's council, or could be offered for entire Congregation Councils.

A schedule similar to the one suggested for congregation retreats might be adapted for synodical use. Synodical leaders could present the material and facilitate group activities. You might want to have people from each congregation work together throughout the workshop, although there is some advantage in mixing groups and letting congregations learn from others' experiences.

While it can be used successfully in a variety of settings, the aim of this book is to help you as a council member find satisfaction in your work on your Congregation Council. It is hoped that as you grow in your understanding of the ELCA and your responsibilities, and as you gain leadership skills, you indeed will find that satisfaction in your ministry.

Chapter 1

THE MINISTRY OF YOUR CONGREGATION COUNCIL

Overview

Using the outline of "Installation of Elected Parish Officers" from *Occasional Services*, the general duties, purposes, and promises of the Congregation Council members will be explored in the light of Scripture's call to mission.

Objectives

Through individual or group study, the participant will:
- Learn that serving as a congregation leader begins with God's call through Holy Baptism.
- Begin to recognize, practice, and appreciate his or her gifts, and those of other council members.
- Grow in the vision of God's mission in the world.
- See his or her ministry on the Congregation Council in the context of God's mission.

Called to Be a Disciple

"I now declare you installed as council members of this congregation. God bless you with his Holy Spirit, that you may prove faithful servants of Christ" ("Installation of Elected Parish Officers," *Occasional Services*, p. 134).

With these or similar words you were or will be installed as a member of the Congregation Council. *Installation* means "the act of putting in place," and you have been "put" in a "place" of ministry as a leader in the church.

But your call to ministry happened before your election to service in your congregation. When you were brought to the waters of life in Holy Baptism, God called you to discipleship and to ministry. It is your Baptism that first put you in your place of ministry. It is your Baptism that continues to empower you for service in Christ's church.

When a congregation welcomes the newly baptized, we affirm: "Through Baptism God has made *these* new *sisters and brothers members* of the priesthood we all share in Christ Jesus, that we may proclaim the praise of God and bear his creative and redeeming Word to all the world" (*LBW*, p. 124).

In Baptism, God commissioned you to ministry within your congregation, and beyond. Your name is joined with the name of the Father, the Son, and the Holy Spirit. You are given new life and a new name. Your new name is child of God: ". . . for in Christ Jesus you are all children of God through faith. As many of you as were baptized into Christ have clothed yourselves with Christ" (Galatians 3:26-27).

The primary ways you express your discipleship to the Lord Jesus are through your relationships (family, friends, work associates) and through your vocation (teacher, farmer, executive, pastor, engineer, carpenter, social worker, health-care worker). In these arenas of everyday life, your discipleship is lived out as you are clothed with Christ.

Most of your ministry is practiced in your relationships and vocations outside the church. But another part of your ministry is expressed within the church, as you labor with others to fulfill the work of your congregation. Your labors will be guided by your Baptism, by the fact that you are a follower of God.

Your Baptism was recalled when you were installed as a leader of your congregation. You were asked to join all the members of your congregation in confessing through one of the creeds "the faith of the Church, the faith in which we are baptized" ("Installation of Elected Parish Officers," *Occasional Services*, p. 133).

The creeds of the church are an expression of the Christian faith, shared by the congregation and its leaders. Your identity as a Christian and the congregation's identity grow out of this common baptismal faith. The Congregation Council is a structure through which this faith is supported and through which your congregation is governed.

Congregation Governance

While the church's creeds have been used by Christians in many centuries and places to express their faith, Christians have not shared a single organizational style. North American churches are organized and governed differently than their counterparts in many parts of the world. Since the early fourth century of the Christian era, when the emperor Constantine made Christianity the official religion of the Roman empire, the churches of Europe usually have been state churches. Such churches have strong ties to the government, and much of their program is subsidized by taxation. The church might be a national church, with congregations or parishes functioning as preaching stations or chapels.

On the North American continent, governments have generally avoided entanglements with religion. Because immigrants who flooded the continent settled as groups in isolated geographic areas, it was natural for them to establish congregations that were essentially independent. North American congregations tend to be organized, therefore, as decentralized, voluntary organizations. People may choose to join or not join congregations of their choice. And each congregation takes responsibility for its own affairs, even to the extent of being separately incorporated and holding title to its own property.

Each Evangelical Lutheran Church in America congregation's constitution and the Congregation Council through which the authority of the congregation is exercised are established to protect the integrity of the congregation's ministry. The constitution and the council safeguard the historical faith and accepted practice of evangelical Lutherans.

Gifts for the Church

Supporting the Christian faith and governing the congregation by carrying out its constitution is a significant responsibility. Fortunately the holy catholic Church, the communion of saints, is a gifted Church. God gives different gifts to different people for the life and mission of the church. During the service of installation, we read from the Apostle Paul:

"Now there are varieties of gifts, but the same Spirit; and there are varieties of services, but the same Lord; and there are varieties of activities, but it is the same God who activates all of them in everyone. To each is given the manifestation of the Spirit for the common good" (1 Corinthians 12:4-7).

The church is equipped by the Holy Spirit with gifts to accomplish its mission. The men, women, and children of the church each are given gifts that are exercised together for the good of the whole.

Offering Your Gift

Imagine that you are part of a leadership team that is starting a new congregation. First decide what gifts you would need from the people working on the team. Make a list of the gifts, and then discuss whether some of those gifts are present in the members of your Congregation Council.

Think about what gifts you as an individual bring to the council. Tell the other members about two of your gifts, and suggest how you can use those gifts to extend your congregation's mission. Finally, as a group talk about ways you can encourage the other members of your Congregation Council to exercise their gifts in ministry.

You might wish to refer to a list or inventory of gifts as you do this exercise together. Several resources are listed at the end of this chapter on page 7.

Challenged with Mission

The ministry to which Jesus Christ has called you will challenge you to share for the gospel's sake all that you have and all that you are.

Form small groups of three or four. Have each group review the Bible passages listed below and identify the challenge for ministry issued by that word. After the groups have finished, note each challenge they identified on a separate sheet of newsprint. On each sheet, list congregation activities that contribute to that ministry in your congregation.

Matthew 28:18-20	Ephesians 4:11-12
Luke 4:18-19	2 Corinthians 4:1-4

The Mission of the Church

The Constitution of the ELCA takes its lead from Scripture, which informs and serves as the ground of our understanding of the church. In groups of two or three, do the exercise "The Mission of the Church" (p. 8). Take a look at the purpose statement in the ELCA constitution and examine its sources in the Bible, matching the scripture passages on the left of the page with the purpose statements on the right. Some of the purpose statements might fit with several of the scripture passages, but there is one that is most appropriate for each statement.

A Mission Statement

If your congregation has a mission statement, read the statement together, and look for the key phrases. What Scripture forms the basis for your mission statement?

If your congregation does not have a mission statement, use your own words to express as a group the mission of your congregation.

Discuss ways your Congregation Council can keep your congregational mission statement before the congregation. Some congregations publish their mission statement on the weekly bulletin or newsletter cover. Others use their mission statement when they are welcoming new members into the congregation. Think about how your congregation expresses and interprets its mission both to its own members and to the community.

Graced with the Promises of God

Your ministry on your Congregation's Council is part of God's mission for the sake of the world. Sometimes we enter into that mission with some reluctance.

Cary York came to church one Sunday because that was what his wife, Sandy, wanted for her birthday. He made it clear that he was going just to make her happy. "I'll come this one time," he said, "but I'll never join the church."

Cary was surprised by how much he enjoyed the congregation's worship and welcome, and several months later, he and Sandy had joined the church. "I'll join the church," he promised his wife, "but I'll never serve on the Congregation Council."

By the time Cary had been a member for several years, his leadership skills had been recognized by the Nominating Committee, and he was elected to serve on the Congregation Council. "I'll serve on the council, but I'll never be the president," he assured Sandy.

You guessed it! Cary York was elected to serve as president of the congregation. In spite of his own intentions, he found himself responding in faith to God's grace, serving as a leader in his congregation.

Cary, like many of us, approached his participation in the congregation reluctantly. But as he was invited to each new way of serving, he found a sense of satisfaction and fulfillment that made it possible to make the next commitment. He was selected for leadership, in spite of his own intentions.

The church has chosen its leaders in various ways through the centuries. In small groups, read Acts 1:21-26 about the way Matthias was selected to be an apostle. Although we might find unusual the method used to choose Matthias, the early church would have understood that God's will was revealed directly through the medium of casting lots, in answer to prayer. Talk about how we select leaders in the church today. How were you selected for this position? Tell your group the story of your invitation to the ministry of leadership.

Promises

The following exhortations are part of the "Installation of Elected Parish Officers":

You are to see that the words and deeds of this household of faith reflect him in whose name we gather.

You are to work together with other members to see that the worship and work of Christ are done in this congregation, and that God's will is done in this community and in the whole world.

You are to be diligent in your specific area of serving, that the one Lord who empowers you is glorified.

You are to be examples of faith active in love, to help maintain the life and harmony of this congregation. (*Occasional Services*, p. 134)

With your agreement to serve on the council, and with the promises you made when you were installed, you pledged to serve as a leader of your congregation. You accepted the duties of a council member as outlined in the installation service. In order to fulfill these responsibilities faithfully, you will need to rely on God to supply the gifts, the grace, and the strength to perform them. God promises to empower us. List the promises from these scripture passages and discuss with your group ways you might have experienced these promises:

Philippians 4:13	1 Corinthians 1:30
Philippians 4:7	2 Corinthians 12:9

The work of the church is God's work. St. Paul observed that our congregations, as with all things human, are merely "clay jars" in which the gospel is contained. It should be clear to us that "this extraordinary power belongs to God and does not come from us" (2 Corinthians 4:7). Although we have imperfections and inadequacies, God still entrusts us with the privilege of being stewards of the good news for all humanity.

This stewardship is both a call and a challenge. God invites each of us to be his partners in ministry. As faithful stewards, in spite of all distractions, we must always give highest priority in our ministry to proclaiming Christ's redemption of the world.

Looking Ahead

- Have a member of your group contact your synod office and ask for a map of your synod. Make a photocopy of the map for each group member. (Some synods might not have maps available.)
- Bring to the next meeting a copy of your congregation's constitution. Before the session, find the sections that refer to the tasks that face your Congregation Council, and circle the number of those provisions in the constitution (for example, C12.04.).

For Further Reading

Bolles, Richard N. *What Color Is Your Parachute?* Berkeley: Ten Speed Press, 1987.

Harbaugh, Gary. *God's Gifted People.* Minneapolis: Augsburg Fortress, 1990.

Hunter, Kent R. *Gifted for Growth.* Church Growth Center, Corunna, IN 46730.

Constitutions, Bylaws, and Continuing Resolutions. Minneapolis: Augsburg Fortress, 1991.

O'Connor, Elizabeth. *Eighth Day of Creation.* Waco, Texas: Word Books, 1971.

Shramm, Mary. *Gifts of Grace.* Minneapolis: Augsburg Publishing House, 1982.

THE MISSION OF THE CHURCH

The Model Constitution for Congregations of the Evangelical Lutheran Church in America describes the Church: "The Church is a people created by God in Christ, empowered by the Holy Spirit, called and sent to bear witness to God's creative, redeeming, and sanctifying activity in the world" (C4.01.). To participate in God's mission, congregations shall, according to the constitution (C4.02.), fulfill many purposes.

Match the Bible passage on the left with the purpose statement from the constitution on the right. Place the letter of the purpose statement in the blank preceding the appropriate passage.

_____ And Jesus came and said to them, "All authority in heaven and on earth has been given to me. Go therefore and make disciples of all nations, baptizing them in the name of the Father and of the Son and of the Holy Spirit, and teaching them to obey everything that I have commanded you. And remember, I am with you always, to the end of the age" (Matthew 28:18-20).

_____ Be united in the same mind and the same purpose . . . (1 Corinthians 1:10) . . . making every effort to maintain the unity of the Spirit in the bond of peace. There is one body and one Spirit, just as you were called to the one hope of your calling, one Lord, one faith, one baptism, one God and Father of all, who is above all and through all and in all (Ephesians 4:1-6).

_____ Let the word of Christ dwell in you richly; . . . sing psalms, hymns, and spiritual songs to God. And whatever you do, in word or deed, do everything in the name of the Lord Jesus, giving thanks to God the Father through him (Colossians 3:16-17).

_____ Hence my eagerness to proclaim the gospel to you also . . . For I am not ashamed of the gospel; it is the power of God for salvation to everyone who has faith . . . (Romans 1:15-16).

_____ As you therefore have received Christ Jesus the Lord, continue to live your lives in him, rooted and built up in him and established in the faith, just as you were taught, abounding in thanksgiving (Colossians 2:6-7).

_____ "I was hungry and you gave me food, I was thirsty and you gave me something to drink, I was a stranger and you welcomed me, I was naked and you gave me clothing, I was sick and you took care of me, I was in prison and you visited me." . . . "Lord, when was it that we saw you hungry . . .?" ". . . Just as you did it to one of the least of these. . . , you did it to me" (Matthew 25:35-40).

a. Worship God in proclamation of the Word and administration of the sacraments and through lives of prayer, praise, thanksgiving, witness, and service.

b. Proclaim God's saving gospel of justification by grace for Christ's sake through faith alone, according to the apostolic witness in the Holy Scripture, preserving and transmitting the gospel faithfully to future generations.

c. Carry out Christ's Great Commission by reaching out to all people to bring them to faith in Christ and by doing all ministry with a global awareness consistent with the understanding of God as Creator, Redeemer, and Sanctifier of all.

d. Serve in response to God's love to meet human needs, caring for the sick and the aged, advocating dignity and justice for all people, working for peace and reconciliation among the nations, and standing with the poor and powerless, and committing itself to their needs.

e. Nurture its members in the Word of God so as to grow in faith and hope and love, to see daily life as the primary setting for the exercise of their Christian calling, and to use the gifts of the Spirit for their life together and for their calling in the world.

f. Manifest the unity given to the people of God by living together in the love of Christ and by joining with other Christians in prayer and action to express and preserve the unity which the Spirit gives.

8

Chapter 2

UNDERSTANDING THE ELCA

Overview
This chapter looks at Scripture, the creeds of the church, and the Constitution of the Evangelical Lutheran Church in America as witnesses to the ministry and vision of the church.

Objectives
Through individual or group study, the participant will:
- Grow in understanding the church by examining Scripture, the creeds, and the ELCA constitution.
- Learn about the ELCA as a church body, with particular structure and purposes.
- Discover the partnership between the congregation, the synod, and the ELCA churchwide organization.
- Receive the challenge to be the church.

The Church
In the liturgy for Holy Communion, we affirm that it is right to give thanks and praise to God "at all times and in all places." The church is the people of God, gathered by God's Holy Spirit from all times and from all places. You affirm with the other members of your congregation that *the church* is located among you. And as Christians we believe that God provides the church in our time and place with gifts of grace and power.

Who is the church? Perhaps you have heard children sing: "I am the church. You are the church. We are the church together. All who follow Jesus all across the world: Yes, we're the church together!"* The pastor declares in the service for Holy Baptism, "By water and the Holy Spirit we are made members of the Church which is the body of Christ" (*LBW*, p. 121). We are the Church, gathered by the Spirit, and called into ministry in Jesus' name.

The Christian church traces its beginnings to one special day in the first century, the day of Pentecost. Pentecost was an ancient festival celebrated by God's people, the Hebrews, 50 days after the Passover. Just weeks after Jesus had died and was raised from the dead, his disciples were gathered together in hiding, fearing discovery, yet waiting for a promise to be kept. Jesus had told them to wait in Jerusalem until they would receive power. Power came! The Holy Spirit changed these waiting ones into a faith community that preached and ministered, witnessed, and grew in numbers every single day. God provided leaders for the church, and much of our New Testament consists of letters written by those early leaders to congregations throughout the Mediterranean world.

Through the centuries the visible institution of Christ's church has been organized in various ways. At several points the church has been fragmented. Lutherans are most familiar with the time of the Reformation in the 16th century, when various denominations of Christians

Avery and Marsh, Volume 1, Hope Publishing

were formed. Even within the worldwide communion known as "evangelical Lutheran" (the largest non-Roman Catholic denomination of Christians), there are many separate organizations and church bodies.

The North American religious scene is especially varied. There are over 200 recognized Christian denominations. The ELCA is the fourth largest, with 11,000 congregations and 5.2 million baptized members. Yet the ELCA is only one of 18 Lutheran church bodies on the continent.

Pictures of the Church
Have you seen a picture of your church building? There are many Bible passages and stories that provide us with pictures of what the church is like. They are like photographs in a scrap book, each telling another part of the story. Read the passages below, and think of a two to three word caption to place under each picture of the church.

Luke 12:32	Ephesians 2:19-22
Romans 1:6-7	1 Peter 2:4-5
1 Corinthians 3:5-9	1 Peter 2:9
1 Corinthians 12:12-26	1 John 3:1

Discuss what each of these images adds to your understanding of the church.

We Believe
The creeds, statements of the faith of the church, also can give us insight into the nature and purpose of the church. The Apostles' Creed describes the church as "the communion of saints." Although you might think that most people in your congregation would not easily fit the common definition of the word *saint*, God's Word says of us that we are indeed "saints" made holy by the death of Jesus (Col. 1:21-22). Martin Luther explained that we are *at the same time saint and sinner* in need of God's saving grace and counted righteous before God.

Another group of people might be united by family or ethnic bonds, vocation, economic status, or even a shared hobby. But the communion into which God places us at our Baptism is formed by the Holy Spirit, who disregards these natural bases for human community and brings together people of all races, walks of life, economic status, and nationalities, and makes them a communion of saints.

The Nicene Creed describes the church in these words: one (calling us to the unity we have with all Christians in every time and place), holy (reminding us that we are set apart by God), catholic (recalling the universal nature of the church), and apostolic (referring to the gospel message as preached by the first apostles).

Another source for study about the church is the Augsburg Confession, the basic Lutheran confession of faith written in 1530, which states in Article VII:

The church is the assembly of saints in which the Gospel is taught purely and the sacraments are administered rightly. For the true unity of the church it is enough to agree concerning the teaching of the Gospel and the administration of the sacraments. It is not necessary that human tradition or rites and ceremonies . . . should be alike everywhere (*BC* 32.1-3).

In recent centuries, groups of Lutherans have adopted purpose statements, developed from Scripture, the creeds, and the Lutheran Confessions. When the Evangelical Lutheran Church in America was formed in 1987, the church adopted as part of its constitution this statement about the nature and purpose of the church:

The Church exists both as an inclusive fellowship and as local congregations gathered for worship and Christian service. Congregations find their fulfillment in the universal community of the Church, and the universal Church exists in and through congregations. . . . In length, it acknowledges itself to be in the historic continuity of the communion of saints; in breadth, it expresses the fellowship of believers and congregations in our day (ELCA 3.02.).

The Power of an Image

How do the descriptions of the church you read above reshape your understanding of the church? Which of these images is most powerful for you? Why?

About the ELCA's Organization

The ELCA constitution affirms that the church functions through congregations, synods, and the churchwide organization, all of which are interdependent. "Each part, while fully the church, recognizes that it is not the whole church and therefore lives in a partnership relationship with the others" (ELCA 8.11.).

These three, then, the congregation, the synod, and the churchwide organization, are all considered to be *expressions* of the Church. All three expressions of the church are guided by the biblical and confessional commitments of the church. All three expressions recognize that mission efforts must be shaped by both local needs and global awareness, by both individual witness and corporate effort, and by both Lutheran emphases and ecumenical cooperation (ELCA 8.16.). Particular responsibilities, however, are assigned to each expression of the church. Each part of the church carries out its responsibilities for the well-being of the whole church and in relation to the other expressions of this church.

It is in the *congregation* that new Christians are brought to the waters of life in Holy Baptism, members are nurtured in a life of discipleship, and the fellowship of faith reaches out to the community in love and service. The congregation's mission, according to the ELCA constitution, includes worship and nurture for its members, and outreach in witness and service to the community (ELCA 8.12.). To this end, the congregation also cooperates with and supports the wider church to strive for the fulfillment of God's mission in the world (ELCA 9.11.).

The church also ministers through *synods*, led by bishops who have primary responsibility for the oversight of pastors, associates in ministry, and congregations within their boundaries. Most of the synods in the ELCA are formed on the basis of geographical areas. Some states where ELCA population is high are divided into several synods. In other parts of the country, ELCA Lutherans in several states join to form a synod.

Synods develop resources for the life and mission of the congregations. Synods certify candidates for ordination, assist congregations with the process of calling pastors, and provide guidance for congregations that have concerns about the ministry carried out in the congregation. When there is a substantial disagreement within a congregation that members cannot resolve, members of the congregation can approach the synod bishop for assistance after informing the Congregation Council chair of their intent (C15.10.). The church's outreach and ministry also are carried out through social ministry agencies, colleges and seminaries, and other organizations. Such ministries are the outgrowth of partnerships between congregations, synods, and the churchwide organization.

Synods are governed by an assembly, which consists of lay representation from each of their congregations and all ordained ministers under call on the roster of the synod. A bishop and a Synod Council are elected to care for the synod's ministries and interpret its mission.

The *churchwide organization* serves on behalf of and in support of the ELCA's members, congregations, and synods. It implements the extended ministries of the church, and organizes for outreach in this country and throughout the world. Churchwide policies, standards for leadership, and criteria for the church's work are developed in consultation with synods and congregations. Resources are shared throughout the church, and programs and services are provided through the churchwide organization. Working relationships are maintained with governmental, ecumenical and social organizations, as well as governmental agencies when necessary.

The churchwide organization is governed by a biennial assembly, with lay and clergy representation from each of its synods. The bishop, vice-president, secretary, Church Council, and boards also are elected to lead the mission of the churchwide organization.

The ELCA constitution states that "congregations, synods, and the churchwide organization are partners that share in God's mission" (ELCA 8.15.). Our partnership through congregation, synod, and the churchwide organization serves to advance the mission of the church for people of all places in our time.

Thinking About Words

The word *congregation* comes from two Latin words meaning "a flock together."

The word *synod* is from two Greek words meaning "a way together" or "coming together."

The churchwide organization serves the ELCA through programs, planning, resources, and coordination. The term *churchwide organization* has been

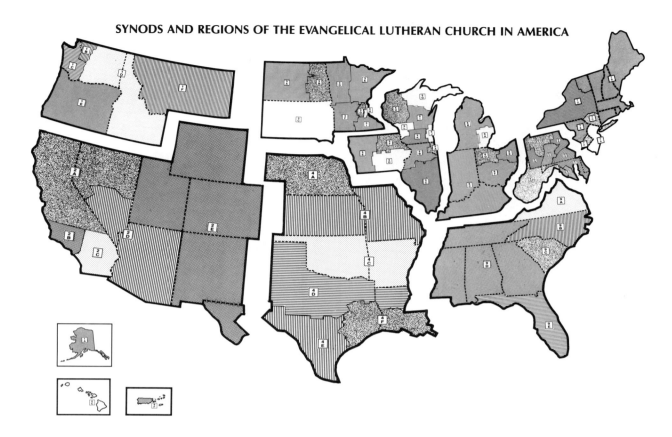

developed by the ELCA to describe this arena of the church's work.

What do the meanings of these three terms, *congregation, synod,* and *churchwide organization,* add to your understanding of the three expressions of the church? How can "a flock together" describe your congregation? What does "coming together" tell you about the purpose of the synodical expression of the church? How does the term "churchwide" expand your vision of the church?

Looking at Maps

Take a look at your synod map and notice the congregations included in your synod. Are there some characteristics that your synod's congregations have in common? Study also the map of the whole ELCA, and notice how the synods and regions are formed.

Our Congregation in Mission

Membership in your congregation through Holy Baptism involves you in this church that extends in mission to all parts of the world, and in ministry to many different ways of serving. In the exercise, "Our Congregation in Mission" (page 12), describe briefly the particular ways your congregation fulfills the purposes of the church as described in the Model Constitution for Congregations.

The Church in Assembly

Have you or anyone from your congregation served as a voting member at a synod assembly or churchwide assembly? Share your impressions about that particular gathering of the church.

Looking Ahead

Bring your copy of your congregation's constitution to your next meeting.

For Further Reading

Dulles, Avery. *Models of the Church.* New York: Doubleday, 1987.

Marshall, Robert. *On Being A Church Member in the Evangelical Lutheran Church in America.* Minneapolis: Augsburg Fortress, 1988.

OUR CONGREGATION IN MISSION

In order to fulfill the purposes of the church, and participate in God's mission, the Model Constitution for Congregations describes the functions of the congregation (C4.03.). After each statement quoted from the constitution, describe briefly the ways your congregation fulfills that purpose. The first statement has been started for you, as an example.

---

a. Provide services of worship at which the Word of God and the sacraments are administered.
    • Church building
    • Worship services
    • Pastoral ministry

---

b. Provide pastoral care and assist all members in participating in this ministry.

---

c. Challenge, equip, and support all members in carrying out their calling in their daily lives and in their congregation.

---

d. Teach the Word of God.

---

e. Witness to the reconciling Word of God in Christ, reaching out to all people.

---

f. Respond to human need, work for justice and peace, care for the sick and the suffering, and participate responsibly in society.

---

g. Motivate members to provide financial support for the congregation's ministry and the ministry of other parts of the Evangelical Lutheran Church in America.

---

h. Foster and participate in interdependent relationships with other congregations, the synod, and the churchwide organization of the Evangelical Lutheran Church in America.

---

i. Foster and participate in ecumenical relationships consistent with churchwide policy.

Chapter 3

DUTIES OF THE CONGREGATIONAL COUNCIL

Overview

A study of the purposes and duties of the Congregation Council takes its lead from the constitutional documents of the church.

Objectives

Through individual or group study, the participant will:
- Examine the duties of the Congregation Council as described in the Model Constitution for Congregations.
- Understand that a call to a position on the Congregation Council is a call to carry out congregation care.
- Explore the concepts of responsibility, authority, and accountability as they relate to the council.

Your Congregation Council

The tasks that face each congregation's leaders are similar, but the way that your council sees itself will shape the decisions it makes. Following are images that describe various leadership teams. These are all legitimate perspectives. Since your council functions in a variety of ways at different times, your council might incorporate several of these images in its self-understanding.

Have group members individually complete the following exercise. Place a plus sign (+) next to the image that describes the way your Congregation Council *prefers* to view itself. Place a check mark (✓) beside the image that *might* describe your council's self-image in some circumstances. Place a minus sign (–) next to the image that is *least* descriptive of your council.

Our Congregation Council sees itself as:
_____ a board of directors for a nonprofit corporation, setting policy and overseeing staff work
_____ a consultant group that advises and suggests policy and direction
_____ a clearing house that gives approval for decisions made by others
_____ elected representatives, accountable to the will of the majority
_____ an advisory body serving as a sounding board for the ideas and interests of the congregation
_____ a core group of the congregation's hard workers
_____ a legislative body, like a city council or town board

As a group, discuss the above exercise, noting similarities and differences in your perceptions of your council.

Council Responsibilities

Many Congregation Council members are not aware that the council is a collective legal personality, similar to a board of directors. Most states require that congregations be organized legally as a corporation or non-profit organization. You as an individual board member have no authority to govern, make commitments, act unilaterally, or supervise staff unless that authority is given to you by the council.

Your congregation's constitution describes your council's responsibilities. It will include statements of faith, the nature of the church, and the purpose of the congregation; descriptions of the congregation's affiliation with the Evangelical Lutheran Church in America; the pastor's responsibilities; and provisions for membership, congregation meetings, committees and other organizations within the congregation, and the discipline of members. Procedures for adopting by-laws and amending the constitution also should be part of your constitution. Every congregation of the ELCA is required to file its constitution with the synod, and the constitution must agree with the constitutions and by-laws of the ELCA and the constitution of the synod. Since your congregation's constitution may be somewhat different from those of other ELCA congregations, this book will refer to the *Model Constitution for Congregations of the Evangelical Lutheran Church in America*, hereafter referred to as "the Model Constitution for Congregations." (Chapters of the constitution referred to most frequently in this resource are printed on pages 47-48.) You should be familiar with your congregation's constitution because it is the Congregation Council's responsibility to see that the provisions of the constitution are carried out (C12.06.).

Congregation Care

If you examined the constitutions from several congregations, you would see certain responsibilities that are assigned to almost every congregation's leaders. Words like supervision, direction, guidance, and management can describe the work of the council. Another way to summarize the work of the council might be: congregation care. The term *congregation care* reminds us that the council's mission and purpose is **relational**. A call to serve as a leader in the congregation is a call to relationship.

The Model Constitution for Congregations refers to the work of the Congregation Council as "oversight of the life and activities of this congregation" (C12.04.). The council's duties can be seen in the major areas of congregation care. The council cares for:
- the congregation's worship
- the congregation's mission
- the congregation's programs
- the congregation's character and climate
- the congregation's partnerships

Caring for the Congregation's Worship

Lutherans see worship as faith in action. The worshipping members proclaim the gospel and celebrate the sacraments. The faithful hear God speak; offer adoration, praise, and thanksgiving to God; and enjoy fellowship with other believers. No matter what other activities the church engages in, public worship is the center of its life and mission. Because the way we worship both reflects and shapes our response to the gospel, how we worship is as important as the fact that we worship.

The Model Constitution acknowledges your Congregation Council's special responsibility for the worship life of the congregation by specifying: "The Congregation Council shall have general oversight of the life and activities of this congregation, and in particular its worship life" (C12.04.). Each of the other aspects of congregation care follow this important priority.

How does your council oversee your congregation's worship life? What can you do to strengthen this element of congregation care? Write your ideas on a large piece of newsprint or on a chalkboard to facilitate discussion. Use the format provided in Appendix A, page 44.

Caring for the Congregation's Mission

Your council exercises congregation care when it "lead(s) this congregation in stating its mission" (C12.04.a.). Caring for your congregation's mission requires that you clearly express that mission and do strategic planning that keeps in mind the purpose of the congregation and the context of your congregation's community. You also will need to evaluate programs and activities in the light of your congregation's mission and goals. Without a clear expression of the congregation's mission, goals, and priorities, members of your congregation will lack a sense of direction, and leadership will falter.

Caring for your congregation's mission is one of the primary responsibilities of congregation care. How does your council assist the congregation in stating its mission? What can you do to strengthen this element of congregation care? You might want to write your ideas on the Congregation Care chart started in the previous section.

Caring for the Congregation's Programs

Your council exercises congregation care when it "seek(s) to involve all members of this congregation in worship, learning, witness, service, and support," and when it "oversee(s) and provide(s) for the administration of this congregation to enable it to fulfill its functions and perform its ministry" (C12.04.b. and c.).

The worship program of your congregation includes lay and pastoral worship leadership, altar care, music provided by choirs and instrumentalists, and hospitality to the stranger. The learning program includes education for children and adults, such as Sunday school, vacation Bible school, and adult Bible study, as well as inservice training for boards, committees, and organizations.

Through the witness program, your congregation shares the good news of the gospel through evangelism, outreach to new members, and care for members who no longer attend worship. The service program includes your congregation's social ministries, the volunteer activities of individual members, and partnership with social service organizations. The support program includes activities that strengthen your members' stewardship.

Administration, overseen by the council, may be carried out primarily by your pastor, a business manager, or members of the parish. The administrator seeks to involve all members of your congregation in its programs, and to coordinate members' service in the programs.

Support and annual evaluation for the **pastor(s)** of your congregation are also important functions of the council. The constitution provides for your council to appoint a Staff Support Committee to maintain supportive relationships with the pastor(s) and staff of your congregation and annually to evaluate their work. It is also the council's responsibility to arrange for pastoral service during the sickness or absence of the pastor (C12.04.g.), and to encourage people from the congregation to consider the ordained ministry as a vocation (C12.04.j.).

How does your council administer its programs and involve all members of the congregation in ministry? Does your council seek to maintain supportive relationship with your pastor(s) and staff through a Staff Support Committee? What can you do to strengthen this aspect of congregation care? You might list your responses on the Congregation Care chart.

Caring for the Congregation's Character and Climate

Serving as a Congregation Council member is not only a matter of public leadership. It is also a matter of personal conduct. The installation service states: "You are to be examples of faith active in love, to help maintain the life and harmony of this congregation" ("Installation of Elected Parish Officers," *Occasional Services*, p. 134). The Model Constitution for Congregations reminds leaders to be examples of the style of life and ministry expected of all baptized people (C12.04.e.).

One responsibility of each council member is to offer hospitality to visitors, keeping nonmembers in mind when making any plans for ministry. Certainly your personal morality should be above reproach. Your personal ethics are also important. For example, as a council member you should avoid problems with conflict of interest, disclosing dual loyalties and refraining from debating or voting on decisions when you have a competing interest. In addition, you should respect confidentiality in your council's decisions, defer to the council's interpretation of decisions, rather than offering your own opinion, and commit yourself to supporting council decisions, even if you did not vote for the decision.

Your council also should be a good example in its corporate behavior. One way the council demonstrates exemplary behavior is by responsibly handling conflict in the congregation. The climate or atmosphere of your congregation is the responsibility of all your members, certainly, but those of you who serve as congregation leaders have a special responsibility to "endeavor to foster mutual understanding" (see C12.04.f.).

When conflicts arise in your congregation, first listen to the complaint, without affirming or denying the validity of the complaint. Then assess the complaint's severity. The council should not be involved in routine organization matters, gossip, or petty trouble-making. The council should be concerned about differences of opinion about the congregation's direction.

Once you are sure you have a clear understanding of the complaint, develop a plan, following your council's policies and procedures for handling complaints. Throughout the process, keep in mind that you do not have authority as an individual to try to resolve substantive issues, but you can demonstrate concern for all involved. Be sure not to make promises to anyone that you might not be able to keep.

If a severe complaint is brought by an employee of the congregation, encourage the employee to follow the established procedures, which should include meeting with the Staff Support Committee. For problems with legal implications, such as alleged sexual harassment, you might meet first with the Staff Support Committee to discuss the situation. Consider asking for help from outside the congregation with particularly difficult situations.

If a complaint comes from a member of the congregation, in most cases you will need to tell the person to discuss the matter with the pastor. Alert the pastor to the problem and the referral, but *not* at a council meeting. The rule is "no surprises." You should expect the pastor to handle the problem from that point, and keep yourself out of the dispute. Only as a last resort should the council or a council committee become involved in resolving complaints.

How does your Congregation Council view its responsibility to be Christian examples? How does your council promote a climate of peace and foster mutual understanding within your congregation? How can you strengthen these aspects of congregation care? In what ways does your Congregation Council consider the stranger in its plans for worship and ministry? Continue to list your responses on the Congregation Care chart.

Caring for the Congregation's Partnerships

Your council exercises congregation care when it helps the congregation work with its partners in mission and ministry. Your congregation ministers with other congregations, the synod, and the churchwide organization. Each partner's mission is expanded because the partners encourage one another. For example, as skilled leaders emerge in your congregation, they can be nominated to serve on synod and churchwide boards and committees. Sharing resources also allows each partner to concentrate on what it does best. Your council also should encourage partnership with non-Lutheran congregations and with other agencies and organizations whose work is in keeping with the goals of the ELCA.

Synods and the ELCA churchwide organization help your congregation fulfill its ministry by providing programs and resources to your congregation. In turn, when your congregation uses these programs and resources, your congregation can work more effectively and experience a sense of identity as an expression of the ELCA. Your council also has an obligation to see that all resources used in your congregation reflect Lutheran theology and doctrine. You should carefully review materials that have not been recommended by this church or published by the church's publishing house.

How does your council support ELCA programs and resources? How does your council emphasize partnership with the synod and churchwide organization? With non-Lutheran agencies and organizations? How can you strengthen this congregation care? Complete the Congregation Care chart.

Looking Ahead
- Bring to your next session a copy of last year's annual report, including the financial report.
- If your congregation has a mission statement, bring the statement to the next session.
- For the next session, have available several years of past annual reports. If reports are available from 10, 15, or 20 years ago or more, bring several of them also.

For Further Reading

Keifert, Patrick. *Welcoming the Stranger: A Public Theology of Worship and Evangelism*. Minneapolis: Fortress Press, 1992.

Lee, Harris. *Theology of Administration: A Biblical Basis for Organizing the Congregation*. Minneapolis: Augsburg Publishing House, 1981.

Chapter 4

FINANCES AND PROPERTY

Overview
This chapter will examine the responsibility of the Congregation Council to manage finances and property.

Objectives
Through individual or group study, the participant will:
- See the congregation budget as a spending plan that sets priorities and gives direction to congregation leaders.
- Understand the role of leaders in managing a congregation's property and finances.
- Hear the biblical call to stewardship of all within our care.

Stewardship
Stewards are managers of resources that belong to someone else. A trustee who manages a trust fund on behalf of someone else is a steward.

The biblical image of a steward reminds us that God has given us all we have and all that we are. We are called to take care of and to share these gifts, to be stewards of our time and talents, our money and possessions, creation, relationships, and God's call to mission. But members of your council are called particularly to be stewards of your congregation's property and financial assets.

Stewards of God's Grace
Read 1 Peter 4:10: "Like good stewards of the manifold grace of God, serve one another with whatever gift each of you has received."

A steward could be thought of as one who "takes care." For what gifts is your Congregation Council the steward? How does your council take care of each of these gifts God has given to and through this congregation?

Congregation Budget
Your congregation probably uses some form of accounting to track its income and expenditures. In fact, your congregation's financial records might be among the oldest records your congregation has. If your congregation is like most, your budget is prepared and presented at an annual meeting. There members review, discuss, and set the budget for the coming year. But even if your congregation does not have a structured annual budget process, it will nevertheless have a spending plan. Your budget then consists of an expectation based on last year's spending record. You probably assume that the bills might increase slightly, but the bottom line figure will remain about the same.

A formal budget or spending plan, however, can be useful to a council. It will help your council plan to spend money according to the wishes of the congregation. A budget is a statement of your congregation's purpose,

since priorities, program goals, and objectives are expressed in the lines of a budget. Finally, a budget provides accountability for finances. When a budget is approved by your congregation, council members are mutually responsible to implement it.

Programmatic Budget
Although your congregation's budget might reflect the congregation's priorities for ministry, a budget also can be deceiving if it is organized by types of expenses. Especially in small congregations, the biggest expenses are probably the pastor's compensation and building expenses. Little money is budgeted for education resources, music ministry, evangelism, and so on. It might appear that the congregation sees these programs as low priority. There is another way to set up a budget, however, to show more accurately how ministries are being supported. In a programmatic budget, the activities of the congregation are grouped into ministry categories, and each expense is related directly to a ministry or service offered by the congregation.

For example, instead of listing worship bulletins under "Supplies," the organist's salary under "Staff Salaries," and choir music and copyright permission costs under "Materials," you can group those items in the category "Worship." In addition, include a percentage of the pastor's compensation (based on the estimated time spent preparing for and leading worship) and of building costs (based on the percent of the building's space used primarily for worship). A programmatic budget for worship might look like this:

Worship ($14,825)

Sunday bulletins	$ 250
Organist salary	2,500
Choir and organ music	300
Copyright permissions	25
Pastor's compensation (25%)	8,750
Building cost (30%)	3,000
	$14,825

The same expenses are listed in both types of budget, but a programmatic budget better reflects the relationship between expenses and the ministries provided. For example, maintaining an older building might not be seen by members as contributing to your congregation's mission. But a programmatic budget makes it clear that building maintenance expenses pay for a place to worship and carry out ministry.

The most important reason to use a programmatic budget, however, is to help communicate the congregation's mission to members. When members of your congregation understand what the congregation is doing and how money is spent, there is a greater commitment to the mission of the congregation.

The following steps can help your Congregation Council develop a programmatic budget.

- Determine several categories that describe your congregation's ministries (for example, worship, learning, witness, service, support).
- Review your previous year's budget and select those items that would be appropriate in each category.
- Combine the expenses for those categories to form a trial programmatic budget.
- Experiment with several different categories and evaluate their effectiveness in interpreting your congregation's ministries.
- Develop the general categories over a period of several years. When congregations first begin using a programmatic budget, the first several budgets will show general categories. The process will become more detailed with time.

Annual Meetings

In ELCA congregations, attendance at annual meetings is often low. Perhaps one reason members do not wish to become involved in this business meeting of the congregation is that they do not see the connection between the business of your congregation and God's mission through the congregation.

Discuss in groups of three or four how your council can help members connect your congregation's budget to your ministry priorities. How can you better interpret your congregation's mission to members? Try to develop specific suggestions.

Other Financial Responsibilities

Records It is important for your council to maintain good records of financial transactions, including copies of insurance coverage, guarantees, personnel and other contracts, and repair schedules.

Memorials If it has not done so already, your council should establish policies and procedures for handling gifts given to the congregation in memory of individuals. The council might recommend projects or programs for support. Recommendations, policies and procedures, and a list of programs and projects supported in the past should be communicated clearly to the congregation.

Assets Your council decides how the financial assets of the congregation will be managed. For example, the council decides whether and how cash should be invested, keeping in mind such possibilities as furthering the mission of the church by investing in the ELCA's mission loan fund, or establishing an endowment.

Insurance Insurance coverage should be arranged for and regularly reviewed by your Congregation Council, in consultation with an insurance carrier.

Cash Reserves Your Congregation Council might establish a contingency fund for emergencies as part of your congregation's fiscal plan. Once cash reserves are adequate to handle short-term emergencies, your congregation probably should devote additional cash on hand to expanded programs, special purchases, or an endowment.

Procedures for Handling Offerings Your Congregation Council has a legal responsibility to ensure that offerings are handled properly. The council also has an ethical responsibility not to tempt people by putting them in a position where they easily could commit a crime. As a general rule, one person (for example, the treasurer) should not be given the responsibility of counting the offering, recording transactions, and writing the checks. At least two people should help count the offering and put it in a safe place before it is deposited in a bank.

All cash and checks should be deposited promptly, and the recordkeeper should make certain the deposit amount balances the checks and cash received. The people who are responsible for recordkeeping should not have access to the mail, and the mail should be opened by someone who is not responsible for recordkeeping.

Proportionate Share

Just as your congregation develops a budgeting or spending plan, your synod and the churchwide organization also develop annual budgets to estimate expenses and income. Your congregation determines the amount of support it will pledge to the wider ministry of the church through synod and churchwide ministries.

The best plan is for your council to appoint a certain percentage of the congregation's total income for this benevolence work. That proportion should be sent regularly (preferably monthly, to assist synod and churchwide planners with their cashflow management) to the synod, which in turn proportionately shares this gift for support of churchwide ministries. One unified gift from the congregation, called "proportionate share," assists in the work of the ELCA through the churchwide organization and the synod. In addition, many congregations designate additional dollars to other ministries such as the World Hunger Appeal or Mission Partners.

Decisions about proportionate share giving are normally made in the congregation's budgeting process, and are approved by the congregation in a congregational meeting. Other decisions about local benevolence or special appeals may be made by the Congregation Council. When your council is making decisions about giving beyond the congregation, you should remember that just as congregation members' growing in their giving allows the ministry of your congregation to be extended, so congregations' growing in their proportionate share each year allows the ministry of the whole ELCA to be extended.

Care of the Congregation's Property and Finances

The concept of congregation care relates to financial and property matters in the congregation. The Model Constitution for Congregations (C12.05.) asserts that among other things it is the council's responsibility:

- To maintain and protect the congregation's property;
- To prepare an annual budget and supervise the expenditure of funds; and
- To give attention to the prompt payment of obliga-

tions and the regular forwarding of benevolence monies to the synodical treasurer.

Your congregation probably has a stewardship or finance committee that develops a stewardship education plan for the congregation, and it is appropriate for your council to delegate stewardship concerns to a special committee. But council members individually and as a group can help strengthen stewardship in the congregation.

First, members of the Congregation Council are leaders in the church. One way for you to lead is by example. The example of leaders who respond to God's generosity, who are committed to the mission of the church, and who support that mission with proportionate giving is compelling to other members of the congregation.

Second, your council should acknowledge that giving patterns have changed significantly in the past decade. People who once contributed to the church out of loyalty now want to have detailed explanations for how their money will be used. Your council needs to help members develop trust by carefully listening to members' concerns and by clearly communicating to members the ways all the expressions of the church exercise their stewardship.

Third, when difficulties arise with your congregation's financial situation, your council should focus on helping members grow in their stewardship and challenging them to support the church's work. Avoid looking for reasons for the problem or blaming a pastor or situation. And remember that even when a congregation is not facing difficulties, it is always appropriate to challenge members to grow in giving. And again, council members can take the lead in accepting the challenge to grow.

In addition to caring for the congregation's stewardship and finances, your council is responsible for maintaining the congregation's building and property. It might be more efficient for your council to form a committee that reports to the council about property concerns. This property committee might oversee building and property repair, preventive and routine maintenance and improvements, custodial personnel, and recordkeeping. A property committee should calculate and arrange for reserves to offset depreciation, determine whether to repair or replace equipment and buildings, and conduct research into new technologies (e.g., telephone systems, computers, video equipment) that might enhance ministry in the congregation. Even if your council has established a property committee, because property stewardship is a matter of congregation care, it is still the responsibility of the entire council. Decisions and recommendations should follow the congregation's constitutional limit on nonbudgeted expenditures (C12.05.c.).

Your Budget Process

In groups of three or four, outline the process by which your congregation determines its annual budget. Are there any changes you might suggest for this process? Does the process reflect the mission statement of your congregation?

Do leaders and other members of the congregation have a solid understanding of biblical stewardship? How could stewardship education in the congregation be improved?

What message do you think your congregation property gives your community about your congregation?

Personal Stewardship

Think about how your understanding of stewardship has prepared you for your work on the Congregation Council. How has your service on the council influenced your personal view of stewardship?

Looking Ahead

For the next session, have available a copy of the most recent congregational report submitted to your synod. Find the membership statistics on the report. How many baptized members does your congregation have?

For Further Reading

Cook, J. Keith. *The First Parish: A Pastor's Survival Guide.* Louisville: Westminster Press, 1983.

Holk, Manfred, Jr. *Clergy Desk Book.* Nashville: Abingdon Press, 1985. See sections on "Maintaining Property and Plant" and "Church Finance and Recordkeeping."

Schaller, Lyle E. *Parish Planning.* Nashville: Abingdon Press, 1971.

Schaller, Lyle E. *The Pastor and the People: Building a New Partnership for Effective Ministry.* Nashville: Abingdon Press, 1973.

Chapter 5

MODELS FOR YOUR COUNCIL'S STRUCTURE

Overview

The Congregation Council needs to consider structural models that are appropriate to the size and context of the congregation.

Objectives

Through individual or group study, the participant will:

- Explore the dynamics of congregational size and context as they relate to the structure of the Congregation Council.
- Examine options for Congregation Council structure.
- Discuss the formation, purposes, and structure of congregation committees.

Organizing the Congregation

"A camel," it is said, "is a horse that was created by a committee!"

However skeptical we might be about the work of committees, it is true that whenever people work together, an organization of some kind begins to develop, and a structure, sometimes including committees, starts to form.

In most congregations, leaders **inherit** a structure. Newer congregations can create new structures that will help the leaders to accomplish the goals of the congregation. Following the formation of the Evangelical Lutheran Church in America, congregations have been encouraged to review their structures and revise their own constitutions. But the task of organizing the church for effective ministry is ongoing, and even if your congregation recently reworked its structure, you might find it helpful to review your work.

If members of your council find themselves wondering, "What's wrong with our organization?" it might be that the organization's structure does not fit the actual dynamics and interrelationships of your congregation's life. If the fit is bad, the structure will not work effectively. For example, a small congregation with nine standing committees might find that there are not enough members to serve on all the committees, and that committee work seems to overlap with work being done by other committees or individuals.

If your council thinks its structure might be hindering its work, you might be hoping to take a new structure off the rack. But there is no single best way to organize for all situations. A tailored version will work much better for your particular congregation. The rest of this chapter should help you determine what that structure is.

Biblical Images

Examine the following biblical images of the church, and discuss the implications of each image for a Congregational Council structure.

Body of Christ (Romans 12:4-5)

Flock (Luke 12:32)
Household of faith (Ephesians 2:19-22)
Vine and branches (John 15:1-17)

Measuring Your Congregation's Size

Several different methods exist for categorizing congregations according to size. Some methods count worshiping members, while others count confirmed members. It can be argued that the number of people who attend worship provides the most accurate characterization of a congregation. If two congregations each have 1000 members, but 200 people on average attend worship in one and 500 in the other, we can be sure the two congregations are different from each other in many ways. For our purposes, however, we will use *baptized* members. Using baptized membership makes it easier to compare congregations of the ELCA, since all ELCA congregations annually report these figures.

Average worship attendance in ELCA congregations is about 30 percent of baptized membership. The percentage varies in different parts of the country and in different size congregations. Look at your own congregation. Is the percentage unusually high or low? Determining membership by counting baptized members also affirms that it is through *Baptism* that a person enters the fellowship of the church and begins a relationship with God and God's people.

At the end of this chapter on page 22 is a chart showing various types or sizes of congregations and some of their characteristics. (This chart is based on the insights of several researchers concerning congregation size and characteristics. Their categories have been adapted to conform to the ELCA categories of congregation size.)

What type of congregation from the chart best describes your congregation's size and context? Check a category, and cross out any characteristics in the description given that do not seem to apply to your congregation. Compare your responses with those of others on your council. As a council, discuss the strengths of your congregation's type.

Tailoring a Structure for Your Congregation

Congregations of different sizes and types have needs for differing organizational structure. Very small congregations often are made up of networks of extended family relationships. There is often an informal power structure totally unrelated to the elected leadership, and those who serve on the council of the congregation might gain from the wisdom of these unofficial, influential leaders.

Very small and small congregations might be informally organized. Decisions made by consensus can be the decisions that will survive. A large number of committees is not practical or helpful. Indeed, small groups from the Congregation Council often can serve as effectively as several committees, or the council of a smaller church can work as a whole to carry out ministry.

Small or moderately small congregations often operate most effectively when their structure recognizes and makes use of the lay leaders. Structures and communication channels should emphasize the connections between committees and the council. Members of very small and small congregations enjoy the opportunity to be part of a close network of caring people. Trying to organize to provide for more programs or simply to be more formal ignores this particular strength of the congregation.

The number and variety of programs that are supported by the medium or moderately large congregation often require a more complex structure, including committees and ministry teams. Planning, supervising, and evaluating programs take coordination and support.

Boards and committees often govern the life of the large or very large congregation. Arranging for volunteer coordination, administering many diverse programs, and making policies and decisions become the responsibility of those selected to serve as congregation leaders.

The context of the congregation is important for determining the type of structure that will best support the congregation's ministry. Congregations that are just getting started will change as they grow from a family-sized church to a larger one. Leaders will need to be responsive to the changes, and it might be necessary to alter the structure as the congregation grows.

Although the strength of small congregations is their network of caring people, in some cases these congregations might benefit from a more complex committee structure that distributes responsibility to more than the few leaders at the center of the congregation.

Large or very large congregations sometimes have within them three or four distinct congregations. Large congregations can take advantage of these divisions within the congregations and support ministry by using a more informal, family church structure if there is good communication between all of the individual groups.

Not all of the characteristics or implications for structure will match your congregation exactly. But the context of a congregation, its size, and its goals are all factors affecting the type of structure that is most appropriate.

Your Congregation's Structure
Make a diagram of your congregation's structure, illustrating the Congregation Council in relationship with the congregation, staff, committees, and organizations. What works? What might you want to change about your organization's structure?

Forming Committees
The Model Constitution for Congregations describes the responsibilities of your council. In order to carry out these responsibilities, your council might form committees or appoint individuals who provide leadership in specific areas. Committees should be specified in either the bylaws or continuing resolutions, rather than in your congregation's constitution. It is easier to alter bylaws or continuing resolutions and therefore to change or eliminate committees that no longer enhance your congregation's ministry. Try to include a sunset provision in your committee structure, and periodically review the need for every committee in your structure. Assume that each committee will be discontinued on a certain date unless your evaluation proves the committee meets an identifiable need.

Constitutional Committees
In addition to committees established by your council, the Model Constitution for Congregations calls for five specific committees.

Executive Committee   The officers and the pastors of your congregation constitute the Executive Committee. Normally this group develops the agenda for council meetings and should regularly discuss how your council is functioning. The Executive Committee can be a good place to test out ideas before bringing them to the full council.

Your council might occasionally delegate some of its routine actions to the Executive Committee, although the council should be careful to retain its authority. When your council refers a task to the Executive Committee, the council should ask the committee to report back when the council's intention has been carried out.

Nominating Committee   While it is elected by the congregation rather than the council, the Nominating Committee is extremely important to the council. Six voting members of your congregation, including two outgoing members of the Congregation Council, are elected to one-year terms at the congregation's annual meeting.

The Nominating Committee helps identify the gifts and skills of potential congregational leaders. Committee members should be familiar with both the members and the leadership needs of your congregation. Committee members should especially look for gifted people who have not served before. And the committee members should have the interpersonal skills needed to recruit the nominees they have selected. (See Appendix B, page 45, for suggested nominating procedures.)

Audit Committee   The Congregation Council must elect annually one of the three members of an Audit Committee, who will serve a three-year term. None of these three people can be a member of the Congregation Council. An Audit Committee may, if members have the skills, audit the financial records itself. Or the committee may work with a volunteer or paid accountant who will carry out this annual task. As the board of directors of the congregation with legal responsibilities subject to your state's laws, your council must be sure that all financial affairs are conducted efficiently and all records kept appropriately. Using noncouncil members to conduct audits makes it unnecessary to assure that people with financial skills are always nominated for the council, and it avoids even the appearance of conflict of interest in the audit process.

Staff Support Committee   The fourth committee required by the constitution is a Staff Support Committee. The council as a whole has the obligation to maintain supportive relationships with the pastor(s) and staff and participate in the annual evaluation of their work. In practice, however, these matters often involve sensitive and confidential discussions. The Staff Support Committee is an appropriate forum for such discussion. The committee also can make recommendations to the council in such matters as position descriptions and performance plans.

The Model Constitution for Congregations calls for a congregation's pastor and president jointly to appoint six members to the Staff Support Committee. Three people are elected each year for a two-year term. Committee members may hold no other office in the congregation during their term in order to be free to play a mediating role when necessary. You might think that six extra people are not available in your congregation. The committee's functions are so important, however, that the constitution specifies that if the committee is not formed, the Executive Committee must serve in this capacity. (See Appendix C, page 46, for a sample job description for a member of this committee.)

Call Committee   One committee is mandated as needed. When a pastoral vacancy occurs, a Call Committee is formed. Whenever a congregation wishes to call a pastor, the first step is to contact the synod bishop for information about the process that will be followed. The synod bishop will offer guidance about how to appoint the Call Committee, which will consist of at least six voting members of the congregation. The purpose of a call committee is to recommend a candidate to a congregational meeting, which will extend a call to a pastor.

Committee Structures

Outside of the constitutional requirements, your council can use whatever structure seems most appropriate. That structure then should be described in your congregation's bylaws. A description of the responsibilities of each committee, task force, or other organization should be contained in your council's continuing resolutions. Here are suggestions for committee structures:

> Establish a coordinator for each ministry, and have the individual organize the work, delegating responsibility and forming work teams as needed. For example, a worship coordinator might work with an altar care committee, music committee, hospitality committee, and ushers. Alternately, you could establish committees for areas of ministry such as worship, witness, learning, service, and support. The four standing committees directed by the constitution (Executive, Nominating, Audit, and Staff Support) also would need to be set up. The coordinator or committee reports to the council but is not a regular member or committee of the council.

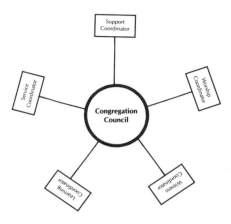

> • Have each member of the Congregation Council serve as liaison to one of the committees, interpreting the mission of the congregation to the committee, and communicating the goals and projects of the committee to the council. The council liaison would report directly to the council, as would the four constitutional committees.

COUNCIL LIAISON STRUCTURE

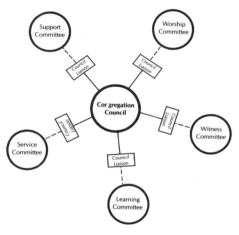

One advantage of forming committees for the work of your congregation is that involving members in committees increases the base of leaders who are committed to the goals of the congregation. As each new committee is formed, however, your council should make sure the expectations and tasks assigned to the group are clear.

The council should provide specific job descriptions for committee members so they know what is expected of them as individuals. (See Appendix C and *Developing Effective Committees* for more about this.)

The council also should describe clearly the relationship the committee has to the council, and to whom the committee is accountable. Committees might report to the council, a staff member or ministry coordinator, or even another committee. Whatever option you choose, make sure the relationship is clear.

In each decision about organization, the mission or purpose of the congregation should be considered. Structure that fits the context of the congregation and its community also needs to serve the mission of the church. Let the structure be a worthy servant of Christ and the gospel.

Looking Ahead

Review the sections in your congregation's constitution that deal with the Congregation Council.

For Further Reading

Callahan, Kennon L. *Effective Church Leadership: Building on the Twelve Keys.* New York: Harper and Row, 1990.

Oswald, Roy M. "How to Minister Effectively in Family, Pastoral, Program, and Corporate Sized Churches." *Action Information,* March/April 1991. Washington, D.C.: Alban Institute.

Olson, Mark A. and Brian Burchfield. *An Evangelizing People: Lay Leadership for a Witnessing People.* Minneapolis: Augsburg Fortress, 1992.

Schaller, Lyle E. *Parish Planning,* "Planning for Our Type Congregation," Chapter 6. Nashville: Abingdon Press, 1971.

Arlin Rothauge. *Sizing Up a Congregation for New Members Ministry.* The Episcopal Church Center, 815 Second Ave., New York.

Rothaar, Michael R. *Developing Effective Committees.* Minneapolis: Augsburg Fortress, 1993.

CONGREGATION CHARACTERISTICS

Size or type of congregation	Characteristics	Implications for organization
VERY SMALL up to 175 members	family congregation with internal leadership networks of extended family relationships	informal power structure might be unrelated to the elected leadership; close network among leaders
SMALL or MODERATELY SMALL 176-500 members	closely knit congregation with intimate fellowship; some emphasis on programming; members have ready access to the pastor	informally organized; decisions made by consensus; small groups from council instead of committees perform tasks; council functions as a whole; lay leaders play important role
MEDIUM or MODERATELY LARGE 501-950 members	highly programmed congregation with active lay ministry	more complex structure; committees and ministry teams provide leadership
LARGE or VERY LARGE over 951 members	corporate, complex congregation with multiple staff, variety of programs	boards govern congregation; staff leadership is primary
IN TRANSITION	changing in membership due to changing community dynamics	congregation needs to adopt organization characteristics for type of congregation it is *becoming*
JUST STARTING	variety in members' experiences and expectations of the church	structure may reflect the experience members bring to the congregation

Chapter 6

YOUR ROLE AS A COUNCIL MEMBER

Overview

This chapter will examine ways congregational leaders work together to carry out their responsibilities.

Objectives

Through individual or group study, the participant will:
- Review the functions of the Congregation Council.
- Study the roles of council members as individuals.
- Understand the concepts of authority, responsibility, and accountability.

Expectations

Once you are elected to serve as a leader of the congregation, you sometimes might feel your task is unmanageable because you do not know what is expected of you. While your congregation no doubt has a number of specific expectations of its council members, generally you should plan on the following expectations:
- Council members should be involved in the congregation, setting the pace and direction of the congregation and building an expectation of excellence.
- Council members should be overseers involved in policy, planning, monitoring, and evaluation. They should not be managers of day-to-day operations.
- Council members should see themselves as question-askers, not answer-givers. Two questions you should ask frequently are "What are we doing?" and "What should we be doing?" Look at what has been happening and evaluate that. Also examine the perceived needs of the congregation, your congregation's strengths and weaknesses, and the challenges and opportunities that are before you.

If you do not know what you are expected to do, you will never know if it was accomplished. Clearly communicated expectations and well-defined roles can help you organize your work and help provide a sense of satisfaction when you complete the task.

Your Council's Structure

Terms   Your congregation's constitution stipulates how Congregation Council members are to be elected and the length of time each council member shall serve. The length of council terms varies from one congregation to another. When your congregation revised your constitution according to the Model Constitution for Congregations, your congregation set a term length.

You are elected to provide congregation care, "general oversight of the life and activities of this congregation" (C12.04.). As a member of the council, you are a representative of the congregation, but you are not elected to represent a particular faction or element of the congregation. You represent and lead the whole congregation. Normally, you will attend meetings of the Congregation Council once a month, but you might attend occasional special meetings, which can be called at the request of the pastor, president, or half of the council's members.

Size   The size of councils also varies from congregation to congregation. A council with nine to sixteen members should be small enough to work efficiently and large enough to avoid overburdening anyone. A council smaller than nine members probably will not be able to fulfill all the responsibilities assigned to it.

A larger congregation will not necessarily require a larger council. In fact, the opposite might be the case. Larger congregations often have more staff members to provide leadership, and the council functions as a policy board. A council that is larger than sixteen members might consider dividing into two boards, an administrative board and a program board, each with distinct responsibilities.

Officers   Members of the council are nominated by the Nominating Committee and elected by the congregation to serve on the council. Four council members also serve the congregation as officers—president, vice president, secretary, and treasurer—of both the congregation and the council.

Officers are elected in various ways. In some congregations, the council elects its own officers from among the council members. These officers then also serve as officers of the congregation for congregational meetings and official representation.

In other congregations, the pastor, who is always a voting member of the council, serves ex officio as president of the congregation and the council. Either the congregation or the council may then elect the other officers. Or all the officers may be elected by the congregation. Officers serve one-year terms, and can serve no more than two consecutive terms.

Officers and the Council

Review together the sections of your congregation's constitution that describe the congregation's officers and Congregation Council, Chapters 11 and 12 of the Model Constitution for Congregations, and any bylaws that might apply.

Responsibility, Authority, and Accountability

Council members' responsibilities are outlined by your congregation's constitution. In addition, responsibilities sometimes are summarized in a job description. Your *responsibility* is what you are expected to accomplish.

As a council member, you are given a job to do by the congregation, which holds ultimate *authority*, expressed through the congregation meeting. Through its constitution the congregation delegates authority to the council to make decisions and to carry out its responsibilities. You are then *accountable* to the congregation. That is, you must give the congregation an account or description of decisions made, plans developed, tasks accomplished, and any problems encountered.

Although the concepts of responsibility, authority, and accountability describe your job as a council member, there are other ways to look at the identity of the Congregation Council. The roles of deacon, trustee, and elder embody the principal tasks assigned to congregation leaders, even though many congregations no longer use these titles.

Traditionally, *elders* care for the spiritual life of the congregation. They may have responsibility for evangelism, visitation of the sick, communication, and community outreach. Those who care for the congregation's property and assets are *trustees*. They may have responsibility for building and grounds, financial stewardship and accounting, office management, and staffing issues. *Deacons* care for the programs that support the members. Deacons may have responsibility for education and Bible study, worship, care of the needy, and for other parts of the congregation's work. Congregations may assign different responsibilities to these three roles, but every congregation needs to make sure that none of the responsibilities is either overlooked or overemphasized.

In *The Management of Ministry,* James Anderson and Ezra Earl Jones describe a parallel for basic leadership tasks. Leadership responsibilities can be divided into three categories: organizational management, associational management, and spiritual direction.

- *Organizational management* is primarily concerned with administration. Responsibilities include managing task groups, building maintenance, fund raising, formal communications within the organization, financial management, and developing organizational procedures. Leaders are charged with providing efficient organizational management.
- *Associational leadership* focuses on conflict management, social leadership, visitation, education, social witness, community outreach, fellowship, and governance, especially as it involves goal setting and consensus formation. These responsibilities all relate to fellowship, and the leaders need to be most concerned with being effective.
- *Spiritual direction* is the work of leaders who provide for religious education, preaching, teaching, counseling, crisis support, prophetic leadership, administration of the sacraments, and prayer and meditation. The unifying concern is faith development, and leaders are called to be authentic.

You can use this model to review the responsibilities assigned to your council by your congregation. Developing a mission statement, strategic planning, setting goals and priorities, and involving members in the congregation's ministries, for example, are associational leadership tasks that need to be carried out in every congregation, no matter what its structure.

Either the trustee/deacon/elder model or the model developed by Anderson and Jones might help your council review its organization to make sure that all areas of responsibility have been appropriately assigned. Or your council can refer to the Model Constitution for Congregations to evaluate its work. Your council may decide to alter any of these models further and determine, for example, that in your congregation a particular leadership task needs to be emphasized to meet a specific need.

At the same time, none of these models is intended to provide a strict division of responsibilities for Congregation Councils. The areas of responsibility are interdependent, and therefore leadership is shared among council members and with the pastor of the congregation. When leadership is not shared, the congregation will not benefit from the training, skills, experience, and perspective of the council and staff as a whole.

Reviewing Your Structure

Review your congregation's constitution, and your council's delegation of assignments and tasks among the council's members and staff. Compare the roles of your Congregation Council with the model developed by Anderson and Jones.

1. Who on your Congregation Council is primarily responsible for organizational management?
2. Who is primarily responsible for associational leadership?
3. Who is responsible for spiritual direction?
4. Do all members of the council take responsibility for all of these leadership tasks?

Satisfaction in Service

Think about what aspects of service and ministry through the Congregation Council are most satisfying to you.

Council Reference Notebook

Each member of the council needs to have ready access to information about the congregation and the council. Some congregations prepare reference notebooks for council members and ask them to pass the notebooks at the end of their terms to the new member elected in their place. You as a council member can use the notebook to help you prepare for council meetings, so business will go more smoothly, and you will feel greater satisfaction as you serve on the leadership team.

Reference material that might belong in a council notebook includes:

Constitutions of the congregation, synod, and churchwide organization
Roster of council members, including addresses and telephone numbers
Copies of reports and minutes from:
- committees
- council meetings
- congregation/annual meetings
- synod/churchwide assemblies

Financial reports
Congregation directory
Job descriptions for:
  • council members
  • committee members
  • personnel
Copies of congregation newsletters

As a group, prepare a table of contents for a council reference notebook that could be used by your council. Ask a recorder to list your ideas.

Looking Ahead
Read 1 Corinthians 12:14-27.

For Further Reading
Anderson, James D. and Ezra Jones. *The Management of Ministry.* New York: Harper and Row, 1978.

Lee, Harris W. *Effective Church Leadership: A Practical Sourcebook.* Minneapolis: Augsburg Fortress, 1989.

Lee, Harris W. *Theology of Administration: A Biblical Basis for Organizing the Congregation.* Minneapolis: Augsburg Publishing House, 1981.

Chapter 7

LEADERSHIP STYLES AND GROUP DYNAMICS

Overview

This chapter examines leadership styles and the interaction between members of the Congregation Council.

Objectives

Through individual or group study, the participant will:
- Explore the variety of leadership styles and consider their implications for leadership in the church.
- Gain confidence in his or her ability to contribute to the group process.
- Learn how to suggest and implement new ideas.

God's Gift of Leadership

Those of you who lead your congregation are given a great responsibility and an awesome challenge. You also are given the gifts of God's Spirit and the companionship of other members along the way.

The leaders congregations elect to the Congregation Council come in various shapes, sizes, colors, and personalities. You each have your own attitudes, ideas, skills, and abilities. You also have certain qualities that set you apart for leadership. In addition, there is another variable among leaders: leadership style.

Before we evaluate several basic leadership styles, it is important to consider first those personal qualities that leaders—like you—bring to the task of leadership.

What Makes a Leader?

Discuss with your group:

What qualities do you look for in a good leader? What personality traits are present in leaders you respect? Have a recorder from your group list on a chalkboard or newsprint the leadership qualities that are suggested by the members of your group.

Qualities of Leaders

One writer refers to four leadership values that contribute to a growing, effective congregation. Perhaps your group has already noted some of these leadership qualities in its discussion:
- a forward-moving spirit of action,
- a sense of compassion and community,
- a clear sense of direction,
- a strong sense of mission in the world.

Other qualities can be identified by a study of biblical leaders. Leaders from the Old Testament, such as Moses, Miriam, Joshua, Deborah, Saul, and David were prized for their decisiveness, wisdom, courage, and for the clarity with which they understood their mission. Compassion was valued, as was a posture of servanthood that served as an example to the nation. In the first century, both the apostle Peter and the apostle Paul wrote letters describing qualities of leaders in the church. Those qualities include gentleness, humility, a willing spirit, and respectability.

But most important is the example of Jesus, who demonstrated the servant leadership that has inspired the church through the ages. In Mark 10:42-45, Jesus spoke about this kind of leadership: "You know that among the Gentiles those whom they recognize as their rulers lord it over them, and their great ones are tyrants over them. But it is not so among you; but whoever wishes to become great among you must be your servant, and whoever wishes to be first among you must be slave of all. For the Son of Man came not to be served but to serve, and to give his life as a ransom for many."

Mark confirmed Jesus' willingness to lead as a servant when he recorded that Jesus took up a towel to fulfill the servant's role and wash the feet of his disciples. The example of Jesus encourages you to see your leadership in the shadow of the cross and to view your leadership as service.

Choosing Leaders

Leadership in the congregation often automatically is given to people simply because they already have exercised leadership in the church. Discuss what would happen if your congregation selected leaders by looking first for people who are decisive, wise, courageous, clear about the church's mission, and committed to service, and then encouraged those people to become leaders.

Styles of Leadership

As individual as our personalities are, each of us also sees leadership in a different way. When we describe styles of leadership, two considerations become quite evident: concern for the task and concern for relationships between people. Some leaders lean toward an emphasis on getting the task done, while others focus on relationship between people. Of course, both of these concerns are important. And when these concerns both are given attention by Congregation Council leaders, more effective leadership will result.

Another aspect of leadership style is the way decisions are made. Some think decisions should be made in a top-down, authoritarian manner. Others see decision making as a consultative process, and still others, as a participatory process.

Styles of leadership can be placed on a continuum, which ranges from authoritarian leadership to total lack of direction by the leader.
- **Top-down:** Leader makes all decisions
- **Consultative:** Leader consults with group(s)
- **Consensus-building:** Leader and group decide together
- **Non-directed:** No leadership, group decides

There probably is no best style of leadership. Leaders and groups need to adapt their styles to fit one another and the situations they face. For example, some emergency situations demand an immediate, top-down decision.

A participatory style of leadership, however, is appropriate for most situations and presents certain advantages. First, it generally results in the group having a greater sense of ownership and a greater willingness to support decisions. It is important to remember that all the members of the Congregation Council have been elected to serve as leaders and probably will want to be included in decisions that affect the direction of the congregation.

Second, a participatory leadership style is appropriate to use in the church because the style is consistent with what we see in Scripture. The Acts 15 account of the Council of Jerusalem deals with a decision the early church needed to make. The story shows how dialogue, listening, and prayer all were used to reach that difficult decision, as church leaders struggled together to be faithful to the will of God. (See Chapter Ten, page 35, for an examination of Acts 15.)

Participatory leadership is also scriptural because it demonstrates trust in the Holy Spirit to work through the different people in the group, producing a wisdom from the whole group.

Discovering Your Own Leadership Style

Working individually, place an "X" on the continuum below, indicating to what degree each concern—for the task or for relationship—is important for you as a Congregation Council member.

Concern for task   Concern for relationship

Next, check the statement below that you think most closely describes the ideal leadership style.

_____ I think there should be one person in charge who makes the decisions for the group.
_____ I think leaders should recommend action but keep in mind the opinions of group members.
_____ I think everyone in the group should talk about the decision and come to an agreement.
_____ I think leaders should let the group decide whatever they want.

Now, as a group match the above leadership style descriptions with the categories: consultative, consensus-building, non-directed, or top-down.

Think about these different leadership styles and discuss the contributions each style would make to your congregation.

The Role of the Congregation Council Member

Every member of your Congregation Council functions in relation to the other members. Decisions are made by the group and implemented by assigning responsibility to individual members. Each council member makes decisions and acts on behalf of the council only as the council has authorized them.

Within the council, there are certain responsibilities that belong to each member:

- Affirm the faith of the church in which we Baptize.
- Attend council meetings and committee meetings as assigned; inform the chairperson and later read the minutes if you must be absent.
- Listen to the congregation; try to become informed about the congregation's life and mission.
- Make yourself familiar with your congregation's constitution and other governing documents.
- Participate in the council's discussions and deliberations.
- Respect the opinions of the other council members.
- Examine the facts of an issue and ask questions if you do not understand.
- Use available experts on an issue, as appropriate.
- Respect the confidential nature of some council decisions.
- Support decisions of the council once they are made; do not encourage dissension by continuing to voice an opposing view to the congregation.
- Remember that the authority to lead is granted by the congregation to the council as a whole, not to you as an individual.

As your council works together, members will begin to serve different functions. One member might help release tension by sharing a sense of humor. Another member might serve as the one who conserves tradition. Another person might serve as reporter for the concerns of the congregation. One might always second motions. And members might begin rely on a certain member to make the motion to adjourn!

Each function might be played by the same persons each meeting, or functions might be exchanged as individuals take part in the interplay that makes a group dynamic and alive. The active participation of each member, however, is important for the health and productivity of the group.

The Body

Read 1 Corinthians 12:14-27 as a group, selecting one member to read the part of the narrator, one to read the foot's part in verse 15, another to read the ear's part in verse 16, and so on. Talk about how this passage is a picture of individuals working together as a group.

New Ideas

At times, responsibility as a Congregation Council member will require you to consider new ideas that might change the future and direction of your congregation. In *Parish Planning*, Lyle Schaller identifies three major sources of new ideas and innovative proposals:

- A crisis that precipitates a response
- An outsider who brings new ideas from another perspective
- The "vision and model concept" (developing a vision in a workshop, conference, or another congregation of what can happen, and studying a model of how the vision has worked in another setting).

When you have a good idea that is new, how can you introduce it and persuade others to accept it? Change happens slowly, especially in institutions, and getting favorable reception of a new idea requires some good groundwork. When you introduce the idea, you should of course be prepared to support and promote the concept, presenting good reasons for the recommended change.

Schaller suggests that your plan to promote an idea include the Four T's:
- Trust: develop a base of trust
- Time: spend time discussing the new idea, and be willing to wait while others catch the vision
- Talk: with supporters and opponents
- Tolerance: be open to diverse proposals for action

Even if your idea is an excellent one and you exercise faithfully each of the Four T's, however, the idea might still be rejected at first. This is a normal reaction to change, and members of almost any organization will respond this way. Sometimes the "no" at first means that the group needs more time to think about the idea.

Realizing that this reaction can be expected can help you avoid becoming disillusioned, or blaming other council members for not accepting your idea. Remember that this initial reaction is part of a group's normal screening process. Continue working on the Four T's, and keep in mind that the group is rejecting the idea, and not you as a person. Consider, too, the possibility that the arguments given for rejecting the idea are good ones. You might want to withdraw the idea, agreeing with the wisdom of the group.

Working Together

Because council members bring their own leadership styles, ideas and opinions, and personalities to the council meetings, it is often difficult to bring about agreement and harmony among the Congregation Council members. But your council faces these challenges because God has given different gifts to your congregation's leaders for the mission to which God calls you.

Personal Leadership Style
Think about some of the influences that have shaped your own personal leadership style. What would you like to change about your leadership style?

Looking Ahead
Complete the "Personal Inventory" (page 31) before the next session, sharing information about yourself through the inventory.

For Further Reading
Greenleaf, Robert K. *Servant Leadership: A Journey into the Nature of Legitimate Power and Greatness*. New York: Paulist Press, 1977.

Lee, Harris W. *Effective Church Leadership: A Practical Sourcebook*. Minneapolis: Augsburg Fortress, 1989.

Chapter 8

BECOMING A LEADERSHIP TEAM

Overview

Building relationships among the members of the congregation's leadership team contributes significantly to the team's effectiveness.

Objectives

Through individual or group study, the participant will:

- Value team building as an essential element for an effective leadership team.
- Explore the dynamics of faith development within the leadership team as team members work together in Christ.
- Recognize the importance of humor and social time in building relationships on the Congregation Council.

Strengthening the Bonds

When members of your council meet for a regular council meeting, you assemble as members of a leadership team. You meet with a promise that upholds you as council members in your work: the promise of Jesus' presence. It is the presence of Jesus Christ that gives meaning to your meetings and purpose to the plans you make together. It is the presence of Jesus Christ that unites the members of your Congregation Council and helps you build an effective ministry team.

In his simple explanation of the work of the Holy Spirit, sent by the Father in Jesus' name (John 14:26), Martin Luther teaches: "The Holy Spirit calls, gathers, enlightens, and sanctifies the whole Christian Church on earth, and keeps it united with Jesus Christ in the one true faith . . ." (Luther's explanation of the Third Article of the Creed).

We are gathered by the Spirit in Jesus' name for important work: to be the church in this time and place. It is the Spirit who calls leaders and gives each one abilities that help the whole body to grow. Leadership teams that recognize the work of God's Spirit and acknowledge the important purpose to which they are called are committed to their Lord, to each other, and to their task.

Evaluating Your Leadership Team

Consider together how effectively your Congregation Council works together. Review and rank these statements, circling the number that best reflects how much you agree with each statement, with 5 the highest and 1 the lowest sense of agreement.

1. I receive a sense of personal satis-   1 2 3 4 5
   faction from my work on the Congregation Council.
2. I enjoy working with the other   1 2 3 4 5
   members of the Congregation Council.
3. Our Congregation Council works   1 2 3 4 5
   cooperatively and succeeds in solv-
   ing problems and making decisions.
4. Members of our Congregation   1 2 3 4 5
   Council communicate well with
   each other; there is room for disagreement and differing opinion.
5. Members of our Congregation   1 2 3 4 5
   Council volunteer to help each other with their tasks.

Now, in groups of three or four, discuss your responses with others on your council. Talk about how you feel about your work with your Congregation Council.

If you have served on the Congregation Council before, tell your small group about the council event, meeting, or program that has been most significant for you. Think about why the experience was important—was it energizing, eye-opening, healing, or significant in some other way?

If you are new to the Congregation Council, tell about a significant experience from another group of which you have been a part.

Listen for common themes in the experiences recalled by your small group. Make a list of the factors that have made these experiences meaningful for you. Tell the rest of the council these factors, and have a reporter write the responses on newsprint or a chalkboard.

What Leaders Can Do

What can the leaders of your Congregation Council do to help your council to work together better as a group? Some "ABC's" of team building are:

- **Appreciate** the members of the team. Pay attention to their work, and acknowledge good work with a good word. People have a need for recognition and esteem, and they can be encouraged by praise.
- **Build** traditions. People have a need to belong, and group memories and traditions can help to build cohesiveness. For example, some councils have a yearly dinner together. Include in your tradition building the opportunity to grow together spiritually through Bible study.
- **Clarify** goals, expectations, and the feelings of the group. Work to set clear goals, and recognize progress toward those goals. Leaders have the responsibility to articulate the mission of the group and to continue to hold the purpose before the group. It also is necessary for the leaders to be aware of the feelings of the group members and to be able to articulate those feelings for the whole group.

- **Delegate** responsibility wisely. People like to have important work to do. Delegate the task to the individual or people on the council best suited for the task, or to those who will enjoy the work most.

What Council Members Can Do

The officers of the council have a special responsibility to foster a sense of cohesiveness on the council, but all the members of the council carry responsibility for nurturing a sense of community within the council to increase the council's effectiveness.

There are several things you can do to help develop that sense of community. First, *contribute* your ideas, especially if there is a diversity of opinion within the council. When your council considers certain issues or concerns, it might even be appropriate for the chairperson to ask each member to voice their opinion. It should not be necessary for everyone to go along with the group in order for the group to get along. Wise decisions depend on all members of the council sharing their opinions.

Consider the viewpoints of others. Respect the other members of your group, and listen for ideas and perspectives that can help you grow in your understanding of the church and its mission.

Demonstrate your *commitment* to support the other members of your council. People who dominate the discussion or try to impose their ideas on the entire group might believe that they are demonstrating their own sense of power. Effectiveness in an organization, however, is developed when the members of the team give power to each other to help the group achieve its aims.

Make an effort to *communicate* openly. Realize that the responsibility to get your point across belongs to you. Express yourself clearly, and try to be patient if the other members do not understand your idea at first. Listen carefully to others' ideas and try to understand them.

Worshiping Together

The single most important element for building relationships on the Congregation Council is developing and strengthening the spiritual dimension. It is God who gathers us together, gives us gifts for ministry, and challenges us with the call to mission. Relying upon the resources of our Christian faith, we can grow in our relationship with God and with each other.

Richard Hutcheson, in *Wheel Within the Wheel*, says, "The wheel within the wheel—the active, moving Spirit of God within the church—is the key to organizational effectiveness." He describes the implications of this principle for leadership in the church, using the church's liturgy and the Bible as resources.

Prayer, he says, is a means of communication within the community. It empowers the community and its members. Groups that pray together are united through that prayer. Your Congregation Council can pray together as you begin your work, taking time to worship together. As you conclude your work, you can pray for individuals or for areas of congregational life. The chairperson or pastor can lead your group in prayer for the community, and members can volunteer petitions. Or, the chairperson can ask first for ideas for petitions and then create a prayer that includes these concerns for the group.

Lutheran Book of Worship offers a variety of excellent resources for worship as a Congregation Council. Some examples are: the evening hymns (*LBW* 272-282), the simplified version (indicated by the small circles) of Evening Prayer (*LBW*, p. 142), or The Litany (*LBW*, p. 168). When your council worships together, the unity you experience in Christ can bind you together, building deeper relationships and helping you grow in your faith.

Participating in the worship life of your congregation is also a responsibility of all Congregation Council members. We grow personally and in Christian community through what Dietrich Bonhoeffer calls our "life together." Our worship together can "make us see our little company as a member of the great Christian Church on earth . . ." (*Life Together*, p. 61).

Council Retreating

Often council members feel there is not adequate time at regular meetings for long-range planning or for developing the unity that the council needs to function well. Overnight or daylong retreats provide the opportunity for a more relaxed and open atmosphere for your council's business. A retreat can give your council time to develop a vision for the future and to grow together through fellowship and learning.

Either a working retreat for planning or self-study, or an inspirational retreat can serve both to build relationships and to develop leadership within your council. You could build a retreat around the handbook *Basic Tools for Congregational Planning* or another leadership resource. *God's Gifted People* by Gary L. Harbaugh or *Selfcare/Wellcare* by Keith W. Sehnert would be suitable for a retreat of a more personal nature. A retreat with a spiritual emphasis could be based on *Celebrating God's Presence* by William E. Hulme, *Life Together* by Dietrich Bonhoeffer, or a Christian classic. Your council could conduct an extended Bible study, or use a retreat structure from *Retreats for Church Groups* or a similar resource. The possibilities are endless.

Social Time

The social dimension of your group needs to be developed and nurtured along with other dimensions. Spending time to get to know each other is an important part of team building. Sharing about home and family, work and play, travel and hobbies can be part of the meeting agenda or can take place during fellowship time before or after each meeting.

When your council understands the importance of social time, it will become easier for your group to schedule time for conversation and team building. Remember that you are not taking time out for social interaction. You are putting time into the group through the trust building, enjoyment, and sense of fulfillment members gain by building relationships with one another.

A Personal Inventory
Use a tool like the "Personal Inventory" below, asking each council member to complete the form before this session. Now have each member share the information with one other person on the council.

Introduce that council member to the rest of the council. Have that council member introduce you, sharing information from the inventory.

Looking Forward
Find the sections in your congregation's constitution that deal with a quorum for council meetings and responsibility for chairing the congregation council.

For Further Reading
Bonhoeffer, Dietrich. *Life Together*. New York: Harper and Row, 1976.

Bormann, Ernest G. and Nancy Bormann. *Effective Committees and Groups in the Church*. Minneapolis: Augsburg Publishing House, 1973. See Part I, "The Dynamics of Good Groups."

PERSONAL INVENTORY

Name _____ Birthday _____

Principal daytime activity _____

Hobbies/leisure activities _____

_____

Roles (husband, wife, parent, daughter, son, student, employee, and so on) _____

_____

Several things I do well and enjoy _____

_____

_____

Experiences I have had with church groups _____

_____

_____

What I think my congregation needs _____

_____

_____

A couple of people who have greatly influenced me _____

Their contributions to my life included _____

_____

_____

I have some gifts, too. Among them are these: _____

_____

_____

Chapter 9

CONGREGATION COUNCIL MEETINGS

Overview

This chapter will examine fundamentals for planning and chairing a meeting with the aim of helping council members to be productive participants.

Objectives

Through individual or group study, the participant will:
- Review different types of meetings, and learn how to determine the best format for each.
- Learn procedures for the effective administration of business meetings.
- Consider the roles of chairperson and pastor in relation to other congregational leaders.

Types of Meetings

A meeting can be defined as any gathering of persons. Listed below are several different types of gatherings. Briefly discuss the purpose of each of these meetings:

Class (to study and learn)	Crowd
Convention	Family reunion
Mob	Conference
Party	Banquet

Calling a Meeting

Meetings can be called for almost any—or practically no—purpose at all. Without meetings, decisions would be made by only one person. Meetings allow groups to share information, discuss ideas, solve problems, develop policies, and maintain the organization.

There are many worthwhile reasons for meeting. But surveys indicate that meetings can also be a significant time-waster. Without a clear purpose for the meeting, gatherings can fall into aimless and fruitless discussion. The first question a Congregation Council or committee member needs to ask before calling any meeting is "Is this meeting necessary?"

You will hold some meetings because your congregation constitution prescribes them. For example, the Congregation Council normally meets once a month. These meetings are required to plan and support ministry, hear reports, make decisions, solve problems, and so on.

Other meetings are called to accomplish a task. Committee meetings, special meetings of the council, meetings of a task force established by the council, social meetings, and informational meetings are examples of meetings often called for a specific purpose. Clearly articulating the purpose of a meeting will help you determine whether the meeting is necessary. Your meeting agenda and format then should be designed to help you achieve the purpose for which you call the meeting.

In a southwestern Iowa community, the local utility board called a "seven-minute meeting." Out of curiosity,

almost every member attended. When they entered the meeting room, they saw a photographer. A picture of the group was then taken for a publicity piece the utility company was planning. "Seven-minute meetings" might not be possible for every purpose, but we might wish that our church meetings could be as focused as that particular board meeting!

Formal and Informal Meetings

Meetings can be conducted formally or informally. Depending on the number of people in your group and the purpose of the meeting, a particular degree of formality might be more appropriate for a given meeting.

Most meetings in a congregation, including Congregation Council and committee meetings, are fairly informal, that is casual and conducted simply. More formal meetings with clear and established procedures and structures, however, actually can help a group function more effectively and free group members to be more relaxed as they conduct their business.

Some aspects of a formal meeting are essential to any meeting. For example, both starting on time and using an agenda will aid you in good time management. When you need to make difficult or controversial decisions, more formal procedures can help ensure that all viewpoints are heard. Groups of more than twelve to sixteen members probably will find that while they can incorporate some elements of informal meetings, they will be more effective using more formal procedures.

Most Congregation Councils will want to try to use the best of both worlds—the simplicity of an informal meeting and helpful structure of a more formal meeting—as fits the needs of the group. All meetings of your Congregation Council, however, bring together two important elements: God's people and God's mission. When leaders work together with a clear focus, either a formal or an informal style can function well.

Efficiency and Effectiveness

Sometimes meetings that are efficient, making wise use of resources, are not effective, accomplishing their goals. Discuss the degree to which you think your council is efficient. To what degree effective? What steps could your council take to become more efficient and more effective?

Meeting Hospitality

When you arrange for a meeting room, keep in mind the basic principle that everyone involved in the meeting needs to be at the same table or in the same circle to feel comfortable and a part of the group.

The limitations of your congregation's facility will determine the flexibility you have to arrange for a meeting. If you think your council members could be more comfortable or feel more a part of the group in a different setting, however, use your imagination. With some creativity you can meet in an area of the church building other than the traditional council meeting space. Or you can arrange the room usually used in a different way.

If your congregation has long tables, arrange them side by side to form a large table top area. Avoid a horseshoe arrangement or putting together four tables so there is an opening in the middle, arrangements that separate people and break the sense of group identity. Placing two long tables end to end also discourages conversation, since people on one end cannot see those on the other end.

Although the size of your Congregation Council might prevent this, meetings can be held in the homes of council members. Meeting in homes takes extra coordination and communication, but it also allows members to get to know one another better. Council members should be free to decide whether they wish to invite your council to their home, since not all council members will feel comfortable making that invitation. Refreshments, if provided, should be kept simple.

Whatever the meeting space arrangements, your goal should be to provide hospitality for those who serve the congregation as leaders.

Procedures for an Effective Meeting

A meeting will be most effective and fulfilling for the council members when:

- Careful planning precedes the meeting. Reports from, for example, the treasurer or a committee should be prepared in advance, preferably in writing. When people with special expertise can add to the meeting, they should be invited to attend to share information or resources with your group. Council members should prepare any assignments they have been given. You might be asked to solicit input from the congregation, to research some matter, or to read an article, perhaps from our church's magazine, *The Lutheran*.
- An agenda has been developed. The agenda should be distributed in advance to the members, if possible, and reviewed by your group at the meeting's beginning.
- The meeting begins on time. If people learn that your council meeting always has a slow start or begins late, they eventually will delay their arrival also. Placing an interesting item at the beginning of the meeting might help members get there on time.

  Sometimes meetings are delayed because a quorum of members is not present. You must have a quorum in order to take formal action. However, you may begin the meeting without a quorum. A quorum is normally half of the members of the group or organization, but your constitution will define a quorum for your meetings. Note that a quorum must include the pastor, except when the pastor requests or consents to be absent.
- Tasks are delegated, so the whole group does not need to deal with all details. Certain tasks can be delegated to individual council members or to another congregation committee.

Making Decisions

Study the following decisions facing a Congregation Council, and place a "CC" on the line before decisions you think the council should make, and an "R" before decisions you think could be referred to a committee, task force, or individual. Discuss your choices with your group. There is not necessarily one correct answer for each item.

—— Make emergency repairs for which the cash is on hand.

—— Conduct a capital fund campaign for major building renovation.

—— Select curriculum for vacation Bible school.

—— Hire staff to run a summer day camp.

—— Add a worship service that uses alternative liturgy.

—— Purchase new choir music.

—— Commit the congregation to sponsorship of a missionary.

—— Decide when to send in designated gifts to the World Hunger Appeal.

Your council, as a rule, should make policy, not establish operating procedures. Discuss a time when your council confused these responsibilities.

The Chairperson and the Executive Committee

The careful planning for every meeting, including preparing the agenda, should involve the person who will chair the meeting. If an elected president will chair the meeting, planning should involve the pastor. If your pastor chairs the meeting, planning should be coordinated and shared with the vice president of the council.

The *executive committee* also might share in planning. The executive committee consists of the pastor and the other officers of the congregation. It might be good for your executive committee to meet before the council meeting to determine the focus of the meeting and to assign specific preparations for the meeting.

When your council meeting begins, the chairperson probably will want to give the group a few minutes to get settled before opening the meeting. The person who was asked to lead worship opens the meeting, and then the chairperson moves through the agenda.

As each item of business is discussed, the chairperson needs to demonstrate respect for each person speaking. When someone presents a proposal, a "second" is needed in order for the group to discuss the proposal. Some kind of response should be made to each statement, however, and the chairperson should follow up if no one else from the group responds. Even if the chairperson and most of the other members do not agree with the speaker, he or she needs to feel that the idea has been heard.

When the discussion about a particular proposal has gone on for some time, the chairperson might sense that it is time to move on and might say something like "Are we ready to make a decision on this?" The chairperson has the responsibility to keep the agenda moving forward, watch the time, keep the group focused on its purpose, study members for indications of frustration or boredom, and use appropriate parliamentary procedure to serve the decision-making process of the council.

Some issues brought before your Congregation Council will need to be presented for action by a congregational meeting, which is the ultimate authority in the congregation. Your council should try to make most decisions, but when an issue must be referred to a congregational meeting, the council as is appropriate should make a recommendation to the congregation.

Part of your chairperson's preparation for any meeting would be to try to anticipate to the extent possible what resources might be needed to answer the questions about a particular agenda item. If the person who chairs the meeting keeps a positive attitude throughout the meeting and encourages good humor and respect toward all of the members of the council, this can set the tone for the meeting and help things to go more smoothly.

The Role of the Pastor

There is variety in the way constitutions prescribe the relationship between pastors and the Congregation Council. When your congregation updated your constitution, you had several options for defining this relationship. These different ways of functioning are outlined in the Model Constitution for Congregations (C11.02.).

Your constitution might indicate that the pastor serves ex officio as president of the congregation and the council. *Ex officio* means "out of the office" or "by virtue of the office." Ex officio does not mean "without voting privileges." If your pastor is ex officio president of the congregation and council, she or he serves in this leadership role by virtue of the office of pastor. That pastor normally would preside at meetings unless this function is delegated. It might be local custom to have the vice president chair the meetings of the Congregation Council, and the pastor chair the annual meeting. A similar arrangement is used in synods, where the bishop presides at the synod assembly, but the synod's vice president chairs the meetings of the Synod Council. If your constitution instead states that the president is elected from the congregation,

the pastor serves as a voting member of the council.

Regardless of which option your congregation chooses for electing officers, there are several council-related tasks assigned to the pastor by the Model Constitution for Congregations. The pastor is to install regularly elected members of your Congregation Council and with the council to administer discipline (C9.03.b.). When your congregation has more than one pastor, each pastor, the Congregation Council, and the synod bishop are expected to consult to develop a document describing the privileges and responsibilities of each pastor. This document accompanies the letter of call.

Generally speaking, your pastor has a responsibility to provide information and guidance on theological issues, although pastors often have input in other matters. A word of caution might be given about the two extremes that can occur—one in which a pastor dominates the workings of the council, not necessarily by words, or the other in which the pastor abdicates responsibility and does not provide leadership. Either extreme destroys the effective working of the council. In this important relationship between the pastor and congregation leaders, it is critical that leadership be shared, clear, open, and non-manipulative.

Looking Ahead

Bring your Bible to the next meeting, and in preparation for the meeting read Genesis 32:6-13, 21-30; 33:1,4; and Acts 15:1-35.

For Further Reading

Bormann, Ernest G. and Nancy Bormann. *Effective Committees and Groups in the Church.* Minneapolis: Augsburg Publishing House, 1973. See especially the chart on pp. 84ff, "If a Group Member Creates a Problem."

Holck, Manfred, Jr. *Clergy Desk Book.* Nashville: Abingdon Press, 1985. See "Managing the Church, Its Organization and Structure," pp. 19-38.

Olson, Mark A. *The Evangelical Pastor: Pastoral Leadership for a Witnessing Pastor.* Minneapolis: Augsburg Fortress, 1992.

Schaller, Lyle E. *The Pastor and The People: Building a New Partnership for Effective Ministry.* Nashville: Abingdon Press, 1973. See especially "Who's in Charge Here?" pp. 111ff.

U.S. News and World Report, December 3, 1973, "How to Make the Most of Your Time."

Chapter 10

MAKING DECISIONS

Overview

Criteria for decision making and methods for working together to make group decisions will be explored in this chapter.

Objectives

Through individual or group study, the participant will:
- Examine criteria for making decisions.
- Consider several methods for decision making, including the process of reaching consensus.
- Learn ways to resolve conflict.

Decisions

Important issues face you as you make leadership decisions for the congregation. Your deliberations require your wisdom, courage, sensitivity, and creativity so that the church can be responsive to the will of God in this time and place. A prayer for guidance begins, "Direct us, O Lord, in all our doings . . ." (*LBW,* p. 49). "All our doings" might begin with the decisions you make as a congregation leader.

Your decisions can reflect hope about a future direction for your congregation's ministry. But your decisions also can reflect the frustration of working with unclear goals and expectations. Your attitude as a congregation leader will shape the way you view your options in decision making. Other factors that will influence the decision-making process include previous experiences that you and members of the congregation have had with the matter under discussion, the complexity of the decision, the number of people who will be affected, and even the structure that is in place for decision making.

Decision-Making Styles

How are decisions made in your Congregation Council? Below are listed ways that congregations make decisions. Check the ones that resemble your Congregation Council's decision-making style.

_____ Extended discussion (Group talks over options until a motion is made that represents the thinking of those who have expressed their opinions. Then the group votes on the matter.)

_____ Consensus (Group agreement emerges from a discussion and a study of alternatives.)

_____ Options (Group chooses from several options, one of which is to affirm the way things are now.)

_____ Vote on proposal (Group makes a decision about a specific motion submitted.)

Discernment

The process of decision making can be informed by the biblical idea of "discernment." When a group needs to discern the will of God, certain criteria can be used to evaluate options and make decisions. These criteria are illustrated by the experience of the early church, which faced a difficult question in the story in Acts 15.

Read the story from Acts 15:1-35 and look for insights that might apply to decision making. The material below is not a critical study of this passage but can be seen as a way to explore and understand decision making.

- When the question became a matter of disagreement, a delegation was appointed to discuss the concern with the apostles and elders, leaders of the church (v. 2).
- Even though debate was certain to follow, the delegation was welcomed by the leaders (v. 4).
- Peter argued from the standpoint of his own knowledge and experience (vv. 7-11).
- The leaders considered the question carefully, and "the whole assembly kept silence, and *listened* to Barnabus and Paul" (v. 12).
- The assembly finally judged the question, discerning God's will by listening to the witness of Scripture (vv. 13-18).
- Their decision was unanimous, as it "seemed good to the Holy Spirit and to us" (v. 28).
- The assembly made plans to implement their decision by sending a return delegation, so that those who were not present when the decision was made could hear directly from among those who participated how the matter was resolved (vv. 22-27).

Of course, the experience of the church in Acts is not meant to suggest a step-by-step approach to decision making or resolving conflict, but it can give you insights into making decisions as a community.

Here are several guidelines for effective decision making that could be adapted and used by your council.

- Clearly define the issue; discuss one issue at a time.
- State the main questions, and work through them.
- Ask group members to contribute their knowledge and skills in the particular area of discussion.
- Consider several points of view and alternatives.
- Maintain respect for every member's opinion.
- Allow time for everyone to understand the issue.
- Make plans to implement the decision.
- Check acceptance and support for the decision.
- Seek the support of persons not present at the meeting.*

Especially remember that when decisions of your council are thought of as opportunities to discern God's will for your faith community, every person's voice and wisdom will be seen as gifts from God.

---

*Adapted from Nathan Turner, *Effective Leadership in Small Groups* (Valley Forge: Judson Press, 1977).

	POPULAR DECISION	UNPOPULAR DECISION
Possible positive result	Peace is kept with family and friends	Decision makers act with integrity, and decision is responsible and sound
Possible negative result	Decision might not be responsible or theologically sound	Relationships might be broken, even if decision is sound

Robert's Rules of Order can help your group formulate resolutions and facilitate the decision-making process. In general, *Robert's Rules* is the standard authority for conducting business. The rules can serve the gospel, too, when your congregation makes decisions. They can help your Congregation Council do its work efficiently and fairly. They also can help insure that decisions are made by the entire council and not by one or two council members. The Model Constitution for Congregations states that *Robert's Rules of Order* govern parliamentary procedure for all meetings of the congregation (C10.07.).

At times, these rules may seem to make the process more complex than it needs to be. But when your council is having trouble making a decision, *Robert's Rules* can protect all those involved in the decision making: the majority, the minority, and even absent members.

When your Congregation Council makes decisions, you should still remember that while parliamentary procedure can certainly be a valuable tool, the fact that members followed parliamentary procedure and voted on a controversial issue does not always resolve the question. When people do not feel ownership of a decision, even if a majority voted in favor of it, the decision might be difficult to implement. But when members of your congregation feel they have had an opportunity to voice their opinions, they are more likely to support the decision, even if they were not involved directly in the decision.

Motions

The aim of decision making is to take action that will help a ministry goal. The first step toward that aim is to propose an action. Making a motion is the most common method by which a particular option is presented for discussion. A motion is a proposal for action, a resolution that favors a particular direction or solution. Motions that are stated positively and clearly have the best chance of being understood by those making the decision. For such motions, a "yes" vote means approval of the action.

In general, two simple rules can help you prepare effective motions:

- State the resolution positively, so that an affirmative vote will approve the proposal. "I move that we establish Stephen Ministries in our congregation."
- Be specific about the subject of the motion and indicate who will be responsible for its implementation: "I move that the Youth Ministry Committee develop a plan for including youth as full members on the boards and committees of this congregation."

Extended Discussion

Provision is made in Robert's Rules for the informal consideration of a question. For example, section 33 states, "While a group is acting informally, every member can speak as many times as he pleases and as long each time as permitted in the assembly. . . ." Many Congregation Councils operate quite well using informal discussion, although extended informal discussion can become inefficient. One advantage of informal discussion, however, is that by the time a motion is made, the discussion might have carried your group to the point where the motion represents the consensus of the group, and a vote simply formalizes the decision.

Reaching Consensus

If your group chooses to use a more structured approach to the consensus process, group members will look for agreement at each point of decision and talk through the decision until consensus is reached within the group. The particular personalities, perspectives, and ideas of each member of your group can add significantly to the shape of the decision as consensus emerges. The major difference between this approach and voting on a motion is that voting seeks to identify the will of the majority, while consensus seeks unanimous agreement. When the consensus process is used, a final decision is made when agreement is reached. A vote at that point can represent an opportunity for affirmation and assent of the proposed action.

Differences of Opinion

Inevitably in the process of making decisions, differences of opinion will arise. Conflict can develop from several sources. Harris Lee, in *Effective Church Leadership*, identifies five basic causes of conflict:

- Personality differences (including conflicting needs and motivations, and actions by antagonists);
- Tension between the two basic goals of the church, to nurture and to reach out;
- Role confusion, usually between pastor and elected leaders;

- Inadequate structure (no written policies, inadequate job descriptions, unclear documents, and so on);
- Inadequate communication, misinformation, or misunderstanding.

Conflict in the Early Church

At the end of Acts 15, studied above, the writer deals with a sharp, unresolved personal issue between Paul and Barnabas that resulted in the two men going separate ways. Although this chapter of Acts gives us insights into decision making, it does not provide a tidy way to deal with conflict between individuals.

In one of Paul's letters, however, he urged the community to help two women who had had a long-standing quarrel. In groups of three or four, read Philippians 4:2-3, and talk about your responsibility, as an individual and as a council, to foster harmony in your congregation.

Strategies for Dealing with Conflict

Harris Lee suggests several strategies to deal with each of the causes of conflict that he identifies, listed above.

- Understanding human nature and practicing tolerance can help in dealing with differences in personality. But according to many of those who work in the area of conflict management, antagonists in the church need to be confronted, called to be responsible in the way they express their opposition, and encouraged to be constructive, not destructive.
- A balanced ministry that takes seriously the twofold purpose of the church will help prevent conflict arising from the tension between nurturing and reaching out.
- Written job descriptions and discussion to clarify roles can help to prevent conflict that arises from unclear expectations.
- A review and discussion of the official documents of the congregation can help leaders clarify the roles of the pastor and lay leaders. Clearly written job descriptions should be prepared and should state to whom each member is accountable. Documents also should be prepared clearly describing the role and responsibilities of the council and committees.
- Making sure that information about goals, program plans, needs, and opportunities is available and that communication is effective can help reduce the opportunity for conflict.

When we deal with conflict in the congregation, we can above all draw upon the many resources of our Christian faith. The gifts of forgiveness and faith draw us into God's peace. This session has presented only one brief summary of one resource that addresses congregational conflict. See "For Further Reading" for other resources.

Jacob and Esau

Read the story of Jacob meeting his brother, Esau (Gen. 32:6-13, 21-30; 33:1, 4). The brothers had been estranged for many years, and Jacob feared for his life as he anticipated meeting Esau. While there are many interpretations of Jacob's wrestling with the stranger, the story points out that blessing can occur even in the midst of conflict.

With what issues has your congregation struggled? How do you see God's blessing for your faith community even when you are involved in a dispute?

For Personal Time

Pray the prayer of St. Francis:
Lord, make us instruments of your peace.
   Where there is hatred, let us sow love;
   where there is injury, pardon;
   where there is discord, union;
   where there is doubt, faith;
   where there is despair, hope;
   where there is darkness, light;
   where there is sadness, joy.
Grant that we may not so much seek
   to be consoled as to console;
   to be understood as to understand;
   to be loved as to love.
For it is in giving that we receive;
   it is in pardoning that we are pardoned; and
   it is in dying that we are born to eternal life.

(*LBW*, p. 48)

Think about how you can be used to share God's peace.

Looking Ahead

- Have available for every council member a copy of the last council meeting's minutes.
- Before the next meeting, review a written copy of the agenda for that meeting.

For Further Reading

Haugk, Kenneth C. *Antagonists in the Church: How to Identify and Deal with Destructive Conflict*. Minneapolis: Augsburg Fortress, 1988.

Leas, Speed B. and Paul L. Kittlaus. *Church Fights: Managing Conflict in the Local Church*. Louisville: Westminster Press, 1973.

Leas, Speed B. *A Lay Person's Guide to Conflict Management*. Washington, D.C.: The Alban Institute, 1979.

Leas, Speed B. *Leadership and Conflict*. Nashville: Abingdon Press, 1982.

Turner, Nathan W. *Effective Leadership in Small Groups*. Valley Forge: Judson Press, 1977.

Chapter 11

PLANNING AND GOAL SETTING

Overview

Working together effectively as congregational leadership requires clear procedures, well-defined goals, and a system for follow-through.

Objectives

Through individual or group study, the participant will:
See the value of careful planning for the meeting.
Understand the purpose of an agenda.
Learn about the goal-setting process.
Consider building evaluation into each of the tasks that face the Congregation Council.

Meetings of the Congregation Council

A productive meeting of your Congregation Council does not just happen. It is the result of planning, preparation, cooperation, and good leadership: that's you!

Often, meetings are criticized for wasting time. Time is money, business says. In the church, time is people, and people are important. Time that council members spend preparing for meetings is an expression of respect for the time of the others in the group.

Your Council's Agenda

Many different elements are part of a Congregation Council's business meeting. Think about your council's last meeting, and place a check beside the items that were part of the council agenda.

____ Reports
____ New ideas discussed
____ Unfinished business reviewed
____ Devotions
____ Budget reviewed
____ Nominations received
____ Recommendations made
____ Policies set

Agenda Building

An agenda is a plan for a meeting. It lists items in the order that they will be considered. An agenda lays out the main purpose for your meeting and lets members of your council know what topics will receive attention. Developing and using an agenda is the first step in turning leadership vision into mission.

An agenda should be prepared by the chairperson of your Congregation Council in consultation with the pastor or another council member. In many congregations, the executive committee regularly meets before the council meeting and develops the agenda for the meetings. Those who will help set the agenda should keep track of items that should come before the council and have the list available when it is time to prepare the agenda. Here is a sample agenda.

RIVERSIDE LUTHERAN CHURCH
Congregation Council Agenda
August 13

Call to Order—Eric Elkin, president
Devotions—Mary Lou Peterson
Leadership Development—Pastor Bradley
Agenda Review
Minutes—Harvey Amundsen, secretary
Treasurer's Report—Edith Paulson, treasurer
Pastor's Report—Pastor Bradley
Committee Reports
    Evangelism—Bud Reese
    Stewardship—Sara Jordan
    Education—James Ivey
    Women of the ELCA—Victoria Walby
    Youth—Karen Solum
Unfinished Business
    Painting the sanctuary
    Other
New Business
    Congregational "Welcome" Booklet
    Other
Visions and Hopes
Announcements, Correspondence
Adjournment

Leadership Development If your Congregation Council spends time near the beginning of each meeting in leadership development, your congregation's leaders can be strengthened through this learning and growing time. For example, reviewing your congregation's mission statement at the beginning of the meeting can help your group keep in mind the purpose of the organization—ministry. Studying the Bible, viewing informational videos, discussing articles and papers, engaging in group building exercises, or focusing on a particular issue all can be ways to develop a Congregation Council.

Agenda Review During the agenda review, council members read through the proposed agenda and make revisions or suggestions. Leaving the agenda open for review can help to build trust on your council by letting members know that their input is valued. This also prevents members from being surprised during the new business portion of your meeting.

Reports Many councils find that turning the agenda around and dealing with business before the reports promotes ministry. If the reports do not relate directly to the business, this arrangement might work well. If your council needs to have information from the committees' reports in order to discuss the unfinished or new business, however, reports might be placed before the discussion of business. Specific action on items included in the reports might be taken during the report or could be handled under unfinished or new business. It might not be necessary for all committees to report at each council meeting.

Visions and Hopes   If your Congregation Council feels free to dream about the future and share its visions and hopes, it might bring change to your congregation. Sharing visions and hopes or brainstorming can create opportunity for new ideas to take shape. It is important that during this visioning time, members make no judgment about the ideas offered. All ideas are welcome and invited.

Sometimes your council might become so overburdened with present concerns and decisions that it does not take time to dream together. Adding brainstorming to the agenda will help make it happen.

Priorities

One important note about setting an agenda: Your council should first give time to matters that have the highest priority. If your council has time after the priority matters have been considered, then it can spend time on other less important items.

Once the agenda is determined, copies should be sent to all the council members so they can see what topics will be considered at the meeting. Seeing the agenda ahead of time allows council members to give matters thought before discussion begins.

Goals, Time Lines, and Objectives

Turning vision into mission requires goal setting. Realistic goals will describe what is to be accomplished. Goals set the sights for the group, so that the resulting action is on target.

Terms like "mission," "objectives," and "goals" often are confusing to people. The mission of the congregation might be expressed in a mission statement, a brief, clear statement about the overall purpose of the congregation.

Goals describe an intended future outcome. Often they begin with a verb that describes what action will be taken.

Here are some examples of goals:
• To provide resources for Christian education.
• To increase worship attendance by 10% next year.
• To study the feasibility of a new congregational social ministry program.

Goals can be specific:
• To provide resources for adult Christian education.

Or even more specific:
• To provide three alternative programs for adult Christian education.

Objectives can be described as minigoals. They are the things that have to happen in order for the goal to be accomplished.

Some objectives might be:
• To select two Bible studies for use in Sunday morning and Thursday evening adult classes.
• To establish an adult forum for Sunday morning to address contemporary issues.

• To organize three fellowship groups that will meet in members' homes.

For some congregations, a detailed plan that includes a mission statement, goals, and objectives will be the best way to turn vision into mission. Your congregation might be uncomfortable with "goal and objective" language, but you still need to be plan for ministry. The goal setting process can be approached in another way. Two questions are at the heart of the goal setting process:
• What do we want to accomplish?
• What do we need to do to accomplish it?

A format like the one below can help your council members visualize a goal setting process based on these two questions.

PLANNING FOR MINISTRY
1. What do we want to accomplish?
2. What steps will we take to accomplish it? (List steps in chronological order.)
   a.
   b.
   c.
3. Who will be responsible for each step?
   a.
   b.
   c.
4. When is each step to be completed?
   a.
   b.
   c.
5. How will we evaluate the project/program?

Your Congregation

Describe the process by which most things get done in your congregation.

If your council does not set goals and objectives, talk about how you could implement such a process and how it would affect your Congregation Council's work.

The Value of Planning

Think about how you use planning in your daily life and work. How can your congregation benefit from planning and follow-through?

Why We Plan

We as members of the church plan for mission to happen, expecting the power of the promised Holy Spirit. We plan, confident that we are working within God's plan: "In Christ God was reconciling the world to himself, not counting their trespasses against them, and entrusting the message of reconciliation to us" (2 Cor. 5:19).

Thomas Campbell and Gary Reierson in *The Gift of Administration* give us these insights about planning:

- The alternative of no planning is even more fraught with unforeseen difficulties.
- The planning process, in spite of its obvious troublesome character, builds community, clarifies "hidden agenda" among the elders, raises expectations, focuses responsibilities, and forms the basis for evaluation and team effort.

Evaluation

An important part of implementing new ideas is to evaluate their success. Compare the results of the project or program to the stated goals and objectives. Did you accomplish what you set out to do? How could the project or program be improved?

An annual review of all of the programs in your congregation might generate ideas about programs and keep current programs on track. Lyle Schaller calls this a "program audit," an annual program review. In a program audit the quality of the work of each committee is evaluated, much as the books are audited for a treasurer's audit. Each committee also can review the job description for committee members and consider how that committee relates to the mission of the congregation.

Taking the time to reflect on your congregation's purpose and how well your congregation is fulfilling that purpose is an important part of the whole process of turning congregational vision into ministry.

Looking Ahead

Bring copies of the following, if they are a part of your congregation's communication strategy, to the next session:

- your congregation's Sunday worship bulletin
- your congregation's newsletter
- a copy of a committee report for your congregation
- a newspaper article about a program in your congregation

For Further Reading

Campbell, Thomas C. and Gary B. Reierson. *The Gift of Administration.* Louisville: Westminster Press, 1981.

Havel, Kirk J. and Michael R. Rothaar. *Basic Tools for Congregational Planning.* Minneapolis: Augsburg Fortress, 1991.

Schaller, Lyle E. *Parish Planning.* Nashville: Abingdon Press, 1971.

Chapter 12

COMMUNICATING WITH THE CONGREGATION

Overview

Maintaining the relationship between a congregation and its leaders can be accomplished in part by good communication, reporting, and listening to the congregation.

Objectives

Through individual or group study, the participant will:
- Examine purposes and methods for recording and distributing minutes.
- Learn to use the reports of committees in the ongoing work of the Congregation Council.
- Explore the communication within the congregation.
- Recognize the importance of listening to the congregation for input into programs and decisions.

Communication Basics

"What's the opposite of talking?" a high level manager asks. The answer many people give, he says, is, " 'Waiting,' waiting for their turn to talk." But it is listening that makes up the other half of effective communication.

Communication involves the exchange of information, but it is much more. Good communication serves to build relationships. Furthermore, relationships facilitate good communication. Of course, communication will happen somehow in your congregation. But if your council wants to responsibly relay information and attend to the congregation's concerns, then communication between your council and the congregation needs to be carefully planned in order to be dependable and effective.

Communication depends on several interrelated dynamics. Every communication involves a sender, a receiver, and a medium. Your Congregation Council, when it relates information to the congregation about decisions and policies, is the sender. To avoid misunderstandings and miscommunication, your council needs to consider the receivers, primarily members of your congregation, and send its messages in a medium and a style that is comfortable for those listeners.

Miscommunication

Think about a time when you heard a rumor about a coworker, neighbor, or family member. Then try to remember an event for which you heard or read continuing news accounts. Finally, remember playing the game "Telephone." In each case, if you were to trace the message you received back to its source, you probably found little resemblance between the final message and the original communication.

Discuss why it is that these situations turn out the way they do. How does miscommunication or relaying misinformation happen in a congregation?

Congregation Council Minutes

When a Congregation Council meets, one of the first items of business is reading the secretary's minutes from the previous meeting. The minutes provide a record of past decisions and provide the context for decisions to be made later. In fact, under correct parliamentary procedure, every decision or policy made by a business meeting remains in effect until the action is completed or changed by another business decision. The minutes of your council communicate the will of the Congregation Council for the future. They also are the channel through which your council speaks as a group and for legal purposes.

Minutes should be as brief as possible, including names, actions, and resolutions. They should show that the action taken was the decision of the group, and not only the responsibility of the person who made the motion. If no action is taken after discussion, the secretary can simply indicate that a topic was discussed.

Often the discussion on a particular issue is complicated, and your secretary will need to clarify the motion or topic to be recorded by reading it back to the group. After the meeting, the secretary should be sure to complete the minutes as soon as possible, so that details are not forgotten and omitted, or incorrectly recorded.

In addition, as your council's decisions are made, a person other than the chairperson and the secretary might be delegated to make notes to assist in followup after the meeting. As each decision is made during the meeting, council members should keep in mind the question "Who needs to know this?" Your council has a responsibility to communicate important council decisions with all individuals, organizations, committees, and the congregation as a whole, according to the interest each has in a particular decision. A form for notations during the meeting might include the following categories:

MEETING FOLLOW UP
Action: New worship bulletins
Person responsible: Jan R.—to order
Date to be completed: 4/2
Who needs to know? pastor, secretary, organist, choir, congregation

---

The appropriate council member may use this format to follow up on specific projects and decisions made by the Congregation Council.

Communicating with the Congregation

The minutes from your council's business meetings could be shared with your congregation on a regular basis. Print a monthly or quarterly meeting digest in your newsletter, publicize that minutes are available upon request, or distribute complete minutes when appropriate.

It is important that your council find ways to share information with the congregation since the only legal way a corporate board such as a Congregation Council can speak is through its actions, the decisions noted in the minutes. Communicating effectively is especially important when the Congregation Council makes an unpopular decision. Your council needs to decide who will be responsible for the communication and make sure its decisions are reported clearly in a number of different ways. It also is critical that your council keep the lines of communication open to listen to the congregation and respond further as needed.

Reviewing Minutes

The minutes of a business meeting can be an important source of information about the past, and much can be learned by reviewing minutes from a period of several years or even decades. Minutes reveal a great deal about a congregation's personality, and by studying minutes, issues that periodically resurface can be anticipated and congregational attitudes can be discovered.

In groups of two or three, study the minutes of a council meeting from the past. If your congregation has been in ministry for many years, study minutes from at least ten or fifteen years ago. Try to identify similarities and differences between the concerns addressed in the past council and in yours today. Talk about ways your council might benefit from the experiences of past councils. Share your learnings with the whole group.

Committee Reports

Committees that have been given responsibility to perform certain tasks are accountable to the Congregation Council. They need to share regularly information about their goals, progress, and needs. Reports from committees are one of the main ways your council receives information. Many actions taken by your council are based on these committee reports. When a committee reports on its consideration of an idea, the council then has a good foundation for its own actions and decisions.

One special report shared with the entire congregation is an annual report. Reports from each committee or organization are included in this report. Budget information and minutes from the previous annual meeting also are included. In addition to summarizing your congregation's activities during the past year, your annual report can help leaders and members evaluate the ministries of the congregation in light of your congregation's goals.

Other reference material could be included in your annual report or in a separate directory. Lists of all committees and organizations with their chairpersons and possibly their members might be helpful for members of the congregation and might serve to facilitate congregational communication.

Annual Report Review

Compare your congregation's annual report with your congregation's mission statement, if one is available. Otherwise, compare your annual report with the purpose statement in the Model Constitution for Congregations (C4.01—C4.05.).

In a small group or together as a council, discuss the following questions:
- What is communicated by our annual report?
- Are we doing what we are supposed to be doing?
- Does the annual report reveal a theme or pattern in our congregational ministry?
- If I were an outsider reading this report, what would I think about this congregation?

Bulletins and Newsletters

Your Sunday bulletin is one of the most useful means of communication within the parish. While the primary purpose of the bulletin is to help people with worship, it also can be used to communicate important announcements. When written from the perspective of a person outside your congregation and without assuming knowledge of the congregation's organizations, ministries, and worship, the bulletin becomes an evangelism tool.

Many congregations have a newsletter to report activities on the congregation's calendar. Your newsletter is a far more appropriate tool than the Sunday bulletin for the communication of Congregation Council business. When the newsletter is mailed weekly, its effectiveness is increased. Programs can be highlighted and thanks can be expressed for the work of committees, individuals, or congregational organizations.

Other Means of Communicating

A telephone network might be useful in your congregation. Posters and bulletin boards are other effective ways for your Congregation Council to share information. These media can effectively utilize pictures to communicate. When you put up a poster or bulletin board, be sure to include the name and phone number of a contact person so people can respond easily to what they see.

Another important contribution to your congregation's overall communication plan might be a congregational brochure or booklet that describes your congregation's worship, program opportunities, or the way the congregation is structured and governed.

When we assume that all visitors will be Lutheran or will have worshiped in a Lutheran congregation before, we miss an important opportunity. We will be failing to listen to the needs of unchurched or non-Lutheran persons who seek an introduction to us and to the way in which we worship. This communication is an essential part of our outreach with the gospel.

Of course, the most effective means of communication is that which is most direct: personal mail or even better, a person-to-person contact. Personal contact not only demonstrates your interest in the person receiving the message. It allows the message carrier to make sure the communication is heard as intended, offering the opportunity for questions and clarification.

Listening to the Congregation

Many methods may be used to listen to the concerns of the congregation. Asking questions is one important aspect of this communication. As a council member, you can ask members of your congregation for their opinions or feelings about a particular topic or issue.

Council members should:

- Listen and ask questions of the members of the congregation.
- Ask for input from the congregation. Brief questionnaires are a structured means of asking for the congregation's ideas. Gathering small groups of people together to study or discuss a particular concern or issue is also a helpful way of discovering the congregation's opinions.
- Remember that listening as a council member is a corporate response. You are not listening as an individual, but instead you are a member of a group of congregational leaders.
- If it is appropriate (and it almost always is), report the ideas and concerns that you hear, relating them to the proper persons or groups.

Congregation members who know their opinions are valued by their leaders feel more a part of leadership decisions, even when they disagree with those decisions.

Communication Checklist

Here is a list of strengths that a lot of councils have. As an individual, review the list and identify your council's strengths and areas that need attention.

Our Congregation Council . . .

____ is interested in suggestions from many congregational members.

____ usually has an open mind when new ideas come up.

____ makes a deliberate effort to seek congregational suggestions.

____ tries hard to implement ideas that come from members.

____ regularly reports its actions (and reasons for them) to the congregation.

____ breaks large problems into small steps that can be acted upon.

____ listens carefully to all council members' points of view.

____ encourages everyone to contribute to all discussions.

____ has members all of whom are active in congregational activities.

____ sees itself as sharing leadership with the pastor(s).

____ spends time together in worship, study, and fellowship.

____ works through problems, rather than avoiding them or trying to fix blame.

____ conducts its meetings from a thoughtful agenda distributed in advance.

____ gathers all the necessary information before voting on an issue.

____ helps its members clarify what each one wants to say.

____ usually looks at all sides of an issue.

____ values the contribution of all, even those who are not as vocal.

____ uses humor to help get through long or difficult sessions.

____ discusses important questions on the basis of Scripture and doctrine.

____ encourages its members to use the gifts they bring from their daily life.

____ sets clear goals and objectives.

____ receives regular reports and updates on work in progress.

____ makes plans in advance and develops church calendar for the year.

____ expects members to speak well of one another and of the congregation.

Discuss your responses in a small group and then report to the whole council for discussion, noting especially any items that might need strengthening in your congregation's communication system.

Your Leadership

As a council member, you lead your congregation in carrying out God's mission. Your call to lead grows out of God's call to you through Baptism. The ministry of your congregation grows out of the witness of Scripture and the creeds, and is given shape by the ELCA constitution. Your responsibility as a council member is to care for your congregation's worship, mission, programs, character and climate, and partnerships. How your council organizes to carry out this ministry may not be the same as the way another congregation does its work. But your council will share the concern of others for using appropriate leadership style, developing as a leadership team, conducting efficient and effective meetings, making well-informed decisions, and planning for ministry. In all your work, you will want to make sure that you communicate well to the members of your congregation, to help them live out their own baptismal call to God's ministry.

For Further Reading

Cook, Keith J. *The First Parish: A Pastor's Survival Manual.* Louisville: Westminster Press, 1983. See "Communications," pp. 61f.

Schaller, Lyle E. *Parish Planning.* Nashville: Abingdon Press, 1971. See "Five Safe Assumptions in Communications," pp. 134-141.

CONGREGATION CARE

1. Caring for our congregation's worship
   What we are doing: *What we can do:*

2. Caring for our congregation's mission
   What we are doing: *What we can do:*

3. Caring for our congregation's programs
   What we are doing: *What we can do:*

4. Caring for our congregation's character and climate
   What we are doing: *What we can do:*

5. Caring for our congregation's partnerships
   What we are doing: *What we can do:*

6. Caring for our congregation's stewardship
   What we are doing: *What we can do:*

SUGGESTED NOMINATING PROCEDURES

Step One

A Nominating Committee of six voting members of this congregation, two of whom, if possible, shall be outgoing members of the Congregation Council, shall be elected at the annual meeting for a term of one year. Members of the Nominating Committee are not eligible for consecutive reelection (C13.02.).

Step Two

The tasks of this committee will vary with the needs of the congregation. The committee could be asked to do any of the following.

- Submit nominees for election to the Congregation Council at the annual meeting.
- Submit names to the Congregation Council for filling vacancies until the next annual meeting.
- Submit nominations for other positions in the congregation, such as education program coordinator, Sunday school or vacation Bible school superintendent, or committee or task force member.
- Review talent and interest survey forms to select persons for leadership and service roles in the congregation.
- Make sure that people are asked to serve when they have volunteered for a task.

Step Three

Suggested procedures for obtaining nominees for the Congregation Council:

- Review congregational membership list for names of persons meeting the requirements of the constitution and the leadership functions and needs of the council.
- Check the talent survey forms for names of those expressing willingness to serve on the Congregation Council or one of its committees.
- Review the names of those who are eligible for reelection to the council.
- Ask members of the congregation, through a bulletin announcement on a previous Sunday, to write the name(s) of possible nominees on a ballot form.
- Contact personally those whose names are recommended most frequently.

Regardless of what method is used, additional nominations from the floor at the time of the election are still to be invited.

Step Four

The Nominating Committee ought to approach each nominee personally, seeking his or her agreement to serve if elected. The interviewer could present the job description, describe the kinds of congregational leaders needed, and outline the help and resources that will be give to the newly elected members. After the interview, the nominee might be given up to a week to pray about, think over, and discuss the opportunity with others. The Nominating Committee might follow up by telephone for the nominee's final response.

Step Five

The Nominating Committee could keep a record of those nominated but not elected. This list would provide names of persons who might fill vacancies as they occur during the year.

APPENDIX C

Sample Job Description for a Member of the Staff Support Committee

Purpose of the Staff Support Committee
The purpose of the Staff Support Committee is to affirm and strengthen the mission of the congregation and the ministry of the staff.

Membership of the Staff Support Committee
The Staff Support Committee is appointed jointly by the president and the pastor. Three persons are to be selected for this committee each year (See the Model Constitution C13.04.).

Responsibilities
The Staff Support Committee:
- communicates expectations and concerns between the congregation and staff
- conducts annual reviews and affirmations of staff
- helps plan continuing education that will benefit congregation and staff
- assesses compensation and benefits provided for the staff

Relationships
The committee is directly responsible to and reports to the Congregation Council.

Time Required
- Attendance at monthly meetings
- Length of term: two years

Qualities of a Committee Member
- Commitment to keeping concerns confidential
- Caring and sensitive
- Able to give constructive criticism

Training Expectations
- Read the handbook *Staff Support Committee: A Vision for Mutual Ministry* by George E. Kech, copyright © 1988 Evangelical Lutheran Church in America.
- Attend synod- or conference-sponsored Staff Support Committee training.

APPENDIX D

MODEL CONSTITUTION FOR CONGREGATIONS
Chapters 11 and 12

Chapter 11.
OFFICERS

C11.01. The officers of this congregation shall be a president, vice president, secretary, and treasurer.
   a.   Duties of the officers shall be specified in the bylaws.
   b.   The officers shall be voting members of the congregation.
   c.   Officers of this congregation shall serve similar offices of the Congregation Council and shall be voting members of the Congregation Council.
   d.   If the Congregation Council elects its officers, the president, vice president, and secretary shall be selected from the elected membership of the Congregation Council.

C11.02. The [congregation] [Congregation Council] shall elect its officers and they shall be the officers of the congregation. The officers shall be elected by written ballot and shall serve for one year or until their successors are elected. Their terms shall begin at the close of the annual meeting at which they are elected.

or

The pastor shall be ex officio president of the congregation and the Congregation Council. The [congregation] [Congregation Council] shall elect by written ballot the other officers of the congregation who shall serve for one year or until their successors are elected. Their terms shall begin at the close of the annual meeting at which they are elected.

or

The pastor shall be ex officio president of the congregation and the Congregation Council. The [congregation] [Congregation Council] shall elect by written ballot the other officers of the congregation who shall serve for one year or until their successors are elected. Their terms shall begin on _____ (month and day) and end on _____ (month and day).

or

The officers shall be elected by the [congregation] [Congregation Council] by written ballot and shall serve for one year. The term shall begin on _____ (month and day) and end on _____ (month and day).

C11.03. No officer shall hold more than one office at a time. No elected officer shall be eligible to serve more than two consecutive terms in the same office.

Chapter 12.
CONGREGATION COUNCIL

C12.01. The voting membership of the Congregation Council shall consist of the pastor(s), the officers of the congregation, and not more than ____ members of the congregation. Any voting member of the congregation may be elected, subject only to the limitation on the length of continuous service permitted in that office. A member's place on the Congregation Council shall be declared vacant if the member a) ceases to be a voting member of this congregation or b) is absent from four successive regular meetings of the Congregation Council without cause.

C12.02. The members of the Congregation Council except the pastor(s) shall be elected by written ballot to serve for _____ years or until their successors are elected. Such members shall be eligible to serve no more than two full terms consecutively. Their terms shall begin at the close of the annual meeting at which they are elected.

or

The members of the Congregation Council [except the pastor(s)] shall be elected at a legally called meeting of the congregation during the month of _____. Their term of office shall be for _____ years with the term of office beginning on _____ (month and day) and ending on _____ (month and day). Newly elected Congregation Council members shall be installed at worship the Sunday prior to the date they assume office.

C12.03. Should a member's place on the Congregation Council be declared vacant, the Congregation Council shall elect, by majority vote, a successor until the next annual meeting.

C12.04. The Congregation Council shall have general oversight of the life and activities of this congregation, and in particular its worship life, to the end that everything be done in accordance with the Word of God and the faith and practice of the Evangelical Lutheran Church in America. The duties of the Congregation Council shall include the following:

a. To lead this congregation in stating its mission, to do long-range planning, to set goals and priorities, and to evaluate its activities in light of its mission and goals.
b. To seek to involve all members of this congregation in worship, learning, witness, service, and support.
c. To oversee and provide for the administration of this congregation to enable it to fulfill its functions and perform its mission.
d. To maintain supportive relationships with the pastor(s) and staff and help them annually to evaluate the fulfillment of their calling, appointment, or employment.
e. To be examples individually and corporately of the style of life and ministry expected of all baptized persons.
f. To promote a congregational climate of peace and goodwill and, as differences and conflicts arise, to endeavor to foster mutual understanding.
g. To arrange for pastoral service during the sickness or absence of the pastor.
h. To emphasize partnership with the synod and churchwide units of the Evangelical Lutheran Church in America as well as cooperation with other congregations, both Lutheran and non-Lutheran, subject to established policies of the synod and the Evangelical Lutheran Church in America.
i. To recommend and encourage the use of program resources produced or approved by the Evangelical Lutheran Church in America.
j. To seek out and encourage qualified persons to prepare for the ministry of the Gospel.

C12.05. The Congregation Council shall be responsible for the financial and property matters of this congregation.
a. The Congregation Council shall be the board of [trustees] [directors] of this congregation, and as such shall be responsible for maintaining and protecting its property and the management of its business and fiscal affairs. It shall have the powers and be subject to the obligations that pertain to such boards under the laws of the State of ____, except as otherwise provided herein.
b. The Congregation Council shall not have the authority to buy, sell, or encumber real property unless specifically authorized to do so by a meeting of the congregation.
c. The Congregation Council may enter into contracts of up to $____ for items not included in the budget.

d. The Congregation Council shall prepare an annual budget for adoption by this congregation, shall supervise the expenditure of funds in accordance therewith following its adoption, and may incur obligations more than $____ in excess of the anticipated receipts only after approval by a Congregation Meeting. The budget shall include this congregation's full indicated share in support of the wider ministry being carried on in partnership with the synod and churchwide organization.
e. The Congregation Council shall ascertain that the financial affairs of this congregation are being conducted efficiently, giving particular attention to the prompt payment of all obligations and to the regular forwarding of benevolence monies to the synodical treasurer.
f. The Congregation Council shall be responsible for this congregation's investments and its total insurance program.

C12.06. The Congregation Council shall see that the provisions of this constitution[,] [and] its by-laws[,] [and the continuing resolutions] are carried out.

C12.07. The Congregation Council shall provide for an annual review of the membership roster.

C12.08. The Congregation Council shall be responsible for the appointment and supervision of the salaried lay workers of this congregation.

C12.09. The Congregation Council shall submit a comprehensive report to this congregation at the annual meeting.

C12.11. The Congregation Council shall normally meet once a month. Special meetings may be called by the pastor or the president, and shall be called by the president at the request of at least one-half of its members. Notice of each special meeting shall be given to all who are entitled to be present.

C12.12. A quorum for the transaction of business shall consist of a majority of the members of the Congregation Council, including the pastor or interim pastor, except when the pastor or interim pastor requests or consents to be absent and has given prior approval to the agenda for a particular regular or special meeting, which shall be the only business considered at that meeting. Chronic or repeated absence of the pastor or interim pastor who has refused approval of the agenda of a subsequent regular or special meeting shall not preclude action by the Congregation Council, following consultation with the synodical bishop.

ISBN 0-8066-1387-4

90000

9 780806 613871

Augsburg Fortress

23-2131